How Did I Get into This Pit?

How Did I Get into This Pit?

Practical Lessons from the Life of Joseph

David Haberer

Pastor Haberer's *How Did I Get into This Pit?* highlights all-too-human experiences with humility. This work offers clarity to shared collective questions and crises faced through relatable terms, examples, and spiritual anchors. This is terrific relaying relatable and extraordinary human weakness and weariness to redemption and salvation
JENNIFER ROSA
Former Events Director of Church For All Nations, NYC

How Did I Get into This Pit? will doubtless stand the test of time and speak to people wanting truth for years to come. This book should be read by everyone.
WILLIAM BONILLA
Virgina Architect

We long for a life that is like a smooth road where we can see where we are going and understand where we've been. The life of Joseph illustrates that God's path for us often leads through difficult relationships, hardships that seem unjust, and times when it seems the Lord has ceased to work good for us. *How Did I Get into This Pit?* gives timely insight on how God guides us on the road of sanctification. As you are led through the story of Joseph, you'll gain hope that the God who worked good from evil for him is also working all things for good for you. And your faith will be strengthened to trust God on the road before you.
BARRY BOUCHILLON
Campus Staff, CRU

As a fifty-year-old who grew up in the Catholic church and wandered away from it as a young adult, and now trying to find the way back, this book hit home on many fronts.

In a time where much of world seems to be missing or ignoring God's message entirely, comfort was found. What I never understood in my younger years has, at times, been even more difficult to understand as an adult. Reading this book brought perspective and insight that I had not anticipated... particularly the plan of God is his plan, not my plan... even when I don't understand it.

By nature, my personality has always been one to question more, not less (the Bible included).

As I continue down my personal faith journey, this book made me feel comfortable with the fact that I won't get every answer to why bad things happen to good people... and that is okay. The stories about real people, struggling in life "going into the pit" for one reason or another, and still trying to live a God-centered life coming out of the pit, even amid all of the confusion in this world, showed me I am not alone.

ROBERT MICHALAK
Recruiter

How Did I Get into This Pit?
Practical Lessons from the Life of Joseph

David Haberer

Copyright © 2024 David Haberer

979-8-9900250-0-4   Hardcover
979-8-9900250-1-1   Paperback

Unless otherwise noted, Scripture quotations are from the ESV® (The English Standard Version®), copyright © 2001 by Crossway, a publishing ministry of Good News Publishers. Used by permission. All rights reserved.

No part of this publication may be reproduced, or stored in a retrieval system, or transmitted, in any form or by any means, mechanical, electronic, photocopying, recording or otherwise, without the prior permission of Journey Faith Media.

Typeset by www.greatwriting.org

Printed in the United States of America

Published by Journey Faith Media

Cover design by Goodwill Media Services

Published in cooperation with Goodwill Media Services, www.goodwillmediaservices.com

Foreword 10
Introduction... 14

SECTION 1: NOT ALWAYS THE BEST PEOPLE 22
Getting the Gospel Right 26
The Call of God... 36

SECTION 2: FROM PIT TO PRISON 46
Did I Really Hear from God? 50
How Did I End up in This Pit? 60
From Bad to Worse 70

SECTION 3: HEALING AND RECONCILIATION 80
Coming Out of the Pit.. 84
What We Have Learned 96

Epilogue: Final Perspectives 106

Dedication

This book is dedicated to my wife, Sharon, who has been my strength for our fifty years of marriage. She is the one who encouraged me to write this book and gave me the confidence to put word to page. Without her support, this book would never happened.

Foreword

Jesus called us to "take up a cross" not to take up a recliner. Some people tell us that the Christian life is all "butterflies and rainbows," but pastor, chaplain, and author, David Haberer, reminds us "Suffering is part of God's process of making us like Christ."

The hymnwriter, Isaac Watts, asks,

> *Must I be carried to the skies*
> *On flow'ry beds of ease,*
> *While others fought to win the prize,*
> *And sailed through bloody seas?*
>
> *Are there no foes for me to face?*
> *Must I not stem the flood?*
> *Is this vile world a friend to grace,*
> *To help me on to God?*
>
> *Thy saints in all this glorious war*
> *Shall conquer, though they die;*
> *They see the triumph from afar,*
> *By faith's discerning eye.*

(Am I a Soldier of the Cross, Isaac Watts, 1721)

David weaves real life stories with the story of Joseph—who goes from pit to prison to palace—and is eventually the instrument of not only saving the people of Egypt from economic ruin, but of also rescuing the brothers who hated him, as well as saving the future nation of Israel.

David reminds us that "when we walk with God, there are times we might find ourselves in a pit." I know that's true. Just as the Lord was with Joseph, he is with you and me, whether we feel lost and abandoned in a pit, forgotten in a prison, or even elevated to a position we never could have imagined. He also reminds us: "When we find ourselves in the pit, we need to press ourselves into the promises of God, for they never change."

As you read this book, I trust God will use it to enable you to trust him more, follow him more closely, and be an encouragement to others who might find themselves in a pit or prison. Don't skip over the *Think About These Things* section. Use this as a time of reflection and prayer. (You might want to even use this in a small group setting.)

Read this book. Pray as you read. I'm sure the God of Abraham, Isaac, Jacob, and Joseph will lift you up, set you free, and restore your joy.

The Rev. Roger D. Haber, D.Min.
Marketplace Chaplains

Foreword

Introduction

We live in confusing times. People are filled with fear and mistrust. It seems that there are more questions than answers, yet they seek simple answers to complex issues. Christians are not immune from life's concerns. How do we know what to do? How do we discern the will of God for life? Can we get a clear answer from God? Can we hear his still small voice and know that he is speaking to us? This is not a new struggle. From the beginning of human history, people have been seeking to discern the will of God.

How It Was in the Beginning

God's intention was to have ongoing fellowship with us. We were created in his image to enjoy a relationship with him, but something happened. Our first parents believed the lie of the enemy. Thinking they could be like God, knowing good and evil, they ate the fruit of the Tree of the Knowledge of Good and Evil. As a result, they were driven from the garden and cut off from the presence of God. Human history is the effort of people to try to reestablish the peace that can only come by restoring the broken relationship with their creator and the unfolding of God's redemptive plan.

Because we are created in God's image, all people are religious and are seeking to make peace with God. Unlike all other religions, Christianity understands that we cannot work our way back to God but rather God, in Jesus, has come to seek us out and draw us to himself. Our role is to engage with God through faith. Scripture tells us the just shall live by faith (see Romans 1:17). That is where our struggle lies. How do we know it is God who is speaking to us and not our own thoughts running through our heads? It's even more difficult than that. Even when we are confident we have heard from God, we cannot always discern his plan—how it will unfold in our life.

Abram's Early Years

Abram is a good example of this kind of struggle. In Genesis 12, God calls him and promises, among other things, to make him a mighty nation. In chapter 15, Abram, in a dream, has a conversion with God regarding the fact that he remains childless. God tells him he will have a son and shows him the stars in the sky, telling him his descendants will be that numerous. We are told Abram believed God and it was counted to him as righteousness. The first step of faith is to believe that you have heard a word from the Lord.

Abram asks God how he will know that God will keep his promise to him. God tells him to prepare a sacrifice, and as the sun goes down God speaks to him again and lays out the plan. Abram's offspring will be captives in a land that is not theirs. They will be afflicted for four hundred years. God will bring judgment upon the nation they serve, and they will come out with great wealth. Abram is told he will live to an old age and die in peace. God then seals the sacrifice for Abram.

Time goes on. Abram knows he has heard from God but still there's no son. He knows the promise, but he doesn't know the plan. He and Sarai come up with their own plan to fulfill God's promise.

Hearing from God

Isn't that how we act sometimes? We believe we have heard from God without knowing the plan, and so we devise our own. God never told Abram how he would accomplish his purposes. All he told him was the promise and he gave some insight into what would take place in the future when Abram would no longer be alive. God speaks to us and shows where we are going and what we are to do, but he leaves out the details. Abram and Sarai decided that, since they were too old to have children, Sari would let Abram have Hagar and she would have a child. Since Hagar was Sarai's servant, she could claim the child as her own. Abram knew the promise, but he didn't know the plan.

Because he was getting old, Abram questioned how God would

keep his promise. He looked at it through natural eyes rather than the spiritual eyes of faith. God did have a plan and it was unfolding as he intended. The plan was for Abram and Sarai to get old, too old to have children, so that when the child was born there would be no doubt in anyone's mind this child was from God. It's in the unfolding of the plan that we must hold on to God.

Abram is not alone in struggling to hold on to God when the plan is not known. Sometimes God reveals the plan but because of our preconceived ideas of how things should work, we miss the plan completely. The disciples walked with Jesus for three years. They heard his teaching, witnessed the healings and the deliverances, the feeding of the multitudes, and even the raising of the dead, and yet they still missed the plan.

How Faith Should Work

At one point Jesus asked his disciples, "Who do men say that I am?" They had many answers, including that he was John the Baptist back from the dead, a prophet etc. Jesus then asked, "But who do you say that I am?" Peter answered, "You are the Christ, the Son of the Living God" (See Mark 8:27-30). Jesus tells Peter he is correct, but it was the Spirit who had revealed that to him. So far, so good.

Jesus then went on to talk about his death and resurrection, but Peter would have no part of it. Jesus rebuked him for listening to the words of Satan. He had faith in Jesus as the Son of God, but his idea of what Messiah would do was incorrect, so he missed the plan of God. Jesus came to establish his kingdom, to conquer sin and death, but the plan was not to come as a ruling king but rather as a suffering servant who would die the kind of death a criminal would—a death in which he was rejected by the Jews at the hands of the Romans. It wasn't until after the resurrection that Peter and the disciples understood how God chose to accomplish his purposes.

The writer of Hebrews tells us, "Now faith is the assurance of things hoped for, the conviction of things not seen" (see Hebrews 11:1-3). He says nothing about the means of reaching God's goal for us. The hope of the church is the New Jerusalem, the city of God coming down from heaven, our eternal dwelling. We have the assurance of faith that this hope is our future reality. We are convinced of it, yet what is the plan to get there? We are being conformed to the image of Jesus, which is the process. Our faith must be rooted in Christ. Like Abram, the promise of God to us is sure. Our faith hangs on God and our belief is that his Word is sure. Our faith is not in events where we have no control over the plan or the process; that is up to God. We have no control over the circumstances of our lives. Our faith is in a God who has complete control.

As Christians we are often caught up in the situation, focusing on what is happening and not on the goal, the promise of where we are going. Our faith is focused on what we are going through and not on the God who orders our steps. So, when things don't seem to be going the way we think they should, we lose hope, our confidence wavers, and our faith falters. Like Peter we cry out, "Let it never be, Lord."

Abram, later renamed Abraham, is called the father of faith. But how can that be? He doubts the ability of God to give him a son through Sarai. Twice, for fear of his own life, he presents Sarai as his sister rather than his wife; he lies. Yet despite these shortcomings, he is known for his faith. How can that be? Peter denies Jesus three times, yet he is used by God in the founding of his church. Faith is not about never having doubts or always seeing things correctly. Abraham is the father of faith because, through it all, he holds on to God. He doesn't always understand what is happening. He is not always sure of God's protection, but he never doubts that God is.

When faith is about controlling situations, it is about us not about God. If God's action is dependent upon our belief, then he is no longer in control. As fallen creatures, we are filled with doubt and uncertainty. We see dimly through the glass of faith. We are challenged constantly to rethink what we believe. Having no control over our circumstances or other reactions, we always second guess what we claim to believe.

What about Job?

Job was a righteous man whose life fell apart because God and Satan were having a war in heaven. Job's friends rebuked him with what seemed to be good, orthodox theology; God rewards the good and punishes the evil, as if to say, "Job, you are suffering because you have done something wrong." They were the ones who lacked understanding. They thought they knew the will of God, and yet it was the friends who missed the mark. Job continually questioned God. At one point he even demanded to present his case before God. What he didn't do was deny God.

Job never got his questions answered, though he did get his life restored. Abraham was the Father of faith because he never let go of God. Despite his sin, he clung on to God. His faith in God was secure.

God's ways are not our ways. As Christians, our struggle is to discern the will of God for our lives—where we are going and what we should do. We search the Scripture for understanding. Often, like Abram, we are not shown how the plan for our lives will unfold. Like the disciples, even when we are told because of our preconceived ideas of what should happen, we miss what God is doing. And sometimes, like Job, we are not told anything at all. If, as the Bible tells us, the just shall live by faith, our responsibility is to trust that God is in control of our lives and he is leading us, even when it seems contrary to our finite understanding.

Dysfunctional Jacob

The story of Jacob is one of a man called by God to save his family, and to move the people of God closer to fulfilling the promise given to Abram—that he would be the father of a mighty nation. Nothing in his life would lead us to believe what God had in store for him and how he would be used by God in his redemptive plan. He comes from a severely dysfunctional family, he is proud and arrogant, and his life path deteriorates as the story unfolds.

There is much to learn about the walk of faith. God's love and direction is seen as he leads Joseph to his appointed end. God moves in mysterious ways and that is clear in this story. If you doubt God can use you because of circumstances in your life, there is something for you in this story. If you don't understand what is happening to you in your life—if things seem to always go wrong or never work out as you planned—consider Joseph's life. And if you think you have heard a word from the Lord, but something is not right, there is a word of encouragement for you here.

Take a journey with me as we follow this Old Testament figure's walk of faith from pampered, spoiled son, rejected by his family, to the second-most-powerful leader in Egypt who is used by God to save the very people who turned against him.

Introduction

Section 1: Not Always the Best People

God's chosen vessels are not always the best people. In fact, many of the great men and women of the faith come from less-than-perfect families. Some of their families are downright broken and dysfunctional. Joseph's is a good example. When he was born, Joseph was the baby of a family of thirteen, twelve sons and one daughter. It would be putting it nicely to say that they did not get along. It's a long and involved story with a jaded past. Let's begin with his father Jacob who would become the father of the twelve tribes of Israel. This broken family was the seed of God's people, the Israelites.

Jacob, the third of the patriarchs of our faith, had a few run ins with his brother Esau. God had called him in the womb to be his chosen servant, but that is no excuse for his behavior. Knowing he was second son and that the birthright belonged to the oldest did not stop Jacob from his pursuit of power. He caught his brother at a vulnerable moment when he was hungry and when he, Jacob, had food. Being the wheeler-dealer that he was, Jacob offered him a bowl of pottage for his birthright. That was not enough for Jacob. When Isaac was near death and his eyesight was failing, he wanted to bless his eldest son, Esau. Jacob wanted no part of that. With the help of his mother, Rebecca, he dressed in a way that he would feel and smell like Esau. He had stolen his birthright and now he had stolen his blessing. Jacob fled to his uncle Laban to avoid the wrath of his brother.

Jacob was God's chosen vessel to advance to promise given to Abraham that would eventually lead to Jesus. He was not the kind of person you would choose to carry forth the glory of God.

Joseph's story doesn't get better. The incidents with his brothers show his true character. God would have to work on him to change him to become the father of the nation that would bring us the Savior of the world. His father, Jacob, met his match in his uncle Laban. He fell in love with Laban's daughter, Rachel. He agreed to work for seven years if Laban would let him marry her. On the wedding night, Jacob got Leah instead. Rachael would cost him seven more years' labor.

Rachel was always the favorite wife, and Jacob did not hide the fact. Things got worse when God closed the womb of Rachel and opened Leah's. Leah kept having children, hoping to win her husband's love. Since Rachel was barren, she gave Jacob her maidservant to have children for her. Leah gave Jacob hers. Back and forth they went, four wives and lots of sons. Finally, Rachel had a son whom she named Joseph. Being the baby and the favorite son, Joseph felt untouchable.

To make the family situation worse, God gave Joseph two dreams that were a glimpse into the future. Joseph saw his family bowing down before him. Not understanding what lay ahead, his brothers were offended, and this added to their hatred of him. Arrogance, sibling rivalry to the extreme, and mothers that were in competition with each other for their husband's love all contributed to the dysfunction of this family, and yet these were the people God would use to carry the promise made to Abraham into the future.

The way God uses us does not depend on where we came from, our family background, or even our personalities. We are all sinners, and we fall far short of the glory of God. Martin Luther tells us that we are sinner-saints. God's use of us is his call. It's always about mercy and grace.

Section 1: Not Always the Best People

1

Getting the Gospel Right

John's Terrible Accident

"Healing is in the atonement." That is what John believed and what he was taught at the church he attended. He had experienced the presence of God in his life, and trusted God would always be there to take care of him. After all, God was his loving Heavenly Father who had only kind intentions toward his children. John was young and healthy; it was easy to believe that if he ever got sick, God would heal him. Isn't that what the Bible says? That was until the accident.

John's accident left him paralyzed from the waist down. He had many struggles those early days in the hospital. He stayed for months at a small local hospital until being moved to a large facility where he could get proper care. It was there he found out that because they had waited too long to move him, he would remain paralyzed. Medical science had done all that was possible, but he still had his faith—and healing was in the atonement.

The accident was decades ago, and his condition has not changed. John was left with a serious dilemma: "Does God exist? If healing is in the atonement and I'm not healed, am I saved. Do I lack faith to believe God's promises?"

The Bible is clear that we are saved by grace. God so loved that world that he took on flesh and lived among us in the man Jesus who died on the cross and reconciled us to God, inviting us to follow him. Martin Luther was clear: we are saved by grace alone, through faith alone, through the Bible alone. The hymn writer said it best,

Nothing in my hand I bring;
Simply to the cross I cling.

John never doubted the existence of God. He did wrestle for a time with the idea that maybe he wasn't saved. After all, he was still not healed—no matter how much he prayed and thought he believed God. He was left with the struggle of faith. If God wants him healed, healing is in the atonement, then the problem must lie with him. Either he didn't believe enough, or he wasn't good enough. There was something wrong with him that was preventing God from healing him.

Seeing from the Right Viewpoint

When we take our eyes off God and view life through our own understanding, we fall back into the first sin. Eve had a choice to make: would she trust God and take him at his word to avoid the forbidden fruit or would she eat the fruit and seek to be like God? Too often we choose the latter. We get the gospel wrong. Our relationship with God is founded on the redemptive work of Jesus. All that we get from God are gifts of grace. Negotiating with God to change a situation in our life is not how we move the hand of God. When we enter a relationship with God based on negotiations, we have fallen into a rabbit hole with no way out. In everything about our relationship with him, from our prayer life to our actions, we are positioning ourselves to move God's hand in our favor to get what we want. John's question was this: "What must I do to receive healing from God?"

When we enter into a relationship with God, we must be aware of two things. The first is that we are dead in our sins. We bring nothing to the relationship. All of our righteousness is as filthy rags before the Father. We are spiritually dead; there is no life within us. Adam was told by God that the day that he sinned he would die. Understanding this is important. Sin is an affront to a Holy God. It is not a mistake or a disease. Sometimes we view sin as an "Oops, I'm bad" situation. But it is much more than that. Sin has broken the relationship we, as a race, once had with God. Our first parents were banned from God's presence because of their disobedience, and that separation remains.

The second thing we need to understand is that the only way to find reconciliation with God is through the death and resurrection of Jesus. Paul tells us that by grace we are saved through faith, and that not of ourselves—it is a gift from God (see Ephesians 2).

These are important truths that we must rightly understand if we are going to face our life struggles. When we look at the life of Joseph, we are aware of his personal sin and the sin of his family. It was dysfunctional in so many ways; his mother, Rachel, and her sister, Leah, did not get along. Two other women were brought into the situation because the sisters were competing for the love of Jacob his father. This led to competition between him and his siblings for their father's attention. Jacob was a man of preferences. He had a favorite wife and a favorite son. Joseph's family was a mess.

Joseph had his own issues. He knew he was the favorite son. He knew his father loved him more than his brothers. After all, he received the coat of many colors. He got to stay home while his brothers went out to take care of the herds. He was boastful of his position in the family and would remind his siblings of it. He received two dreams from God in which his brothers and his parents bowed before him. He didn't know the meaning of the dreams, but he let them know he was going to somehow rule over them.

God Chooses to Use Sinners

What I love about the Scriptures is that they pull no punches. God doesn't hide from us the sins of those who went before us. Joseph was chosen by God to be the instrument by whom he would save his family and move forward the promise he made to Abraham. Joseph and his family were not the kind of people I would think God would choose to carry out his divine plan, as they were not model citizens. But that is the point: God chooses people like Joseph and like you and me to accomplish his plan of redemption. God chooses sinners. His using us cannot depend on our good works. If it did, he could use no one because none of us is worthy. Salvation is by grace alone. If God can use Joseph, God can use you.

Often our struggles are based in a misunderstanding of the gospel. There is no negotiating with God. Our relationship with him is based on grace. All that we get from God is undeserved. We can't negotiate with God for a better deal. "If you do this, I'll do that. . ." That's the response of sinners. "God get me out of this mess I'm in, and I will serve you." It's based on the idea of penance. If I do the right something, then God will be appeased, and he will grant me my wish. It is not the gospel but it is a common response when we find ourselves in a situation beyond our control. It is rooted in the idea that somehow I, through my actions, can move the hand of God. I can be like him. That very idea is contrary to the reality that we are dead in our sins and cannot please God.

When we don't get the gospel right, it affects our sense of self-worth. When we are in situations we can't change or control and God doesn't answer our prayer, the reaction often is to blame ourselves. "There must be something wrong with me, so that's why God has left me in this situation." The tendency is to feel unworthy. There is a human need to feel wanted, to have value. If we feel that God is avoiding us, not answering our prayers, not delivering us from life's struggles—small or great—we are left with and internal struggle. "God is not answering because he does not exist; God is not answering because I am not worthy of his care." At times like this the enemy presses in, suggesting you can be like God. "If God does not exist, you are on your own. If God is avoiding you, then you are on your own." The need to feel worthy drives us to seek it elsewhere.

When Eve was confronted with the lie that she could be like God, she acted. She saw the fruit as the means to self-worth and control of her life. When we question God, we are forced to look in other places to meet our need to feel worthy. The world is quick to offer alternatives.

The creation account is clear: we are made in the image of God. David the psalmist reminds us that we are fearfully and wonderfully made. Our self-worth is found in our creation. It is not found in what we do, but in whose image we are made after. The redemption story should solidify our sense of self-worth. God loved us so much that he sent Jesus to redeem us from our sinful state and adopt us into the family of God. Jesus taught us to pray, "Our Father who art in heaven. . ." (Matthew 6:9-13). Our standing with God never changes, no matter what condition we might be in or what struggles we may face. Nothing can separate us from the love of God. But when we lose sight of the gospel and begin to doubt God's love, we no longer have a foundation for grounding our worth in God. It's at that point that we look to the things of this world to assure us that we are good enough—and then God will be pleased with us and finally answer our prayer.

The world honors and rewards success. The person who exceeds financially is looked up to and respected as someone in power. Too often, churches buy into these ideas and adopt them into their understanding of God. If you are right with God, he will bless you. If you are struggling financially or suffering with an illness that is not cured, that must mean that God is not pleased with you. If you come from a dysfunctional family, if you are in any way disabled, or sick, it must be evidence of God's displeasure and you are disqualified from being used by him. It was the argument of Job's friends and one often heard in Christian circles—God blesses the righteous and punishes the wicked. If you are sick and struggle, your family is a mess, poor, or any one of a million situations people find themselves in, then you are seen as being of no use to God. When it is spoken in the church, it becomes devastating to the individual. However, there is no basis in the Bible for this belief.

Seeing with God's Eyes

It turns out that Job's friends were wrong. They had no understanding of what had taken place in heaven. Paul, who was used by God to heal people, suffered from an affliction he prayed for deliverance from and was denied by God and told his grace was sufficient. Jacob wrestled with God and his leg was put out of joint, leaving him to hobble as he walked. There were reasons for all these conditions. God does nothing by accident or chance. Job's friends had to be taught not to judge what they had no understanding of. Paul was humbled; what he accomplished was the work of God. Jacob was reminded that he wrestled with God. In each of these situations, the people involved were drawn back to God and forced to lean upon him. Too often, we seek to get out of situations when what we really need to see is God at work in our lives for our good and for his greater purpose. Paul reminds us that God is in every situation, working for the good of those who love him and are called according to his purposes (Romans 8:28, 29).

Joseph was a spoiled young man. His life was centered on his privileged position as his father's favorite son. He walked in confidence and he let his brothers know where he stood with their father. Jacob would send Joseph to check up on his brothers and he would bring back bad reports. His dreams of dominance added to the family division. If that wasn't bad enough, he paraded himself in an expensive, multicolored coat his father had made for him.

Joseph's dreams were nevertheless from God. Jacob who was not pleased with them and he still hid these thoughts in his heart. He, from experience, knew that God might be in the dreams. This was not the best person and not the best family, yet God was at work and God would use all of them. This family was the foundation of the nation of Israel. God would use them in the carrying out his plan of redemption.

When we lose focus on the work of God in our lives, we end up groping around in the dark, searching for things that cannot satisfy. The world offers what it cannot deliver. The promise to be like God, knowing good and evil, could not bring life. Eve's reach led to death. Our whole economy is built of promises of false hope. "Wear these clothes, drive this car, live in this neighborhood, and you will be happy and whole," we are told by the secular media. The Christian version of the media tells us: "Serve God perfectly and he will bless you with health and prosperity. Don't engage in certain behaviors, and all of life problems will be solved."

Why do we seek after false gods, and why do we look for satisfaction and self-worth in other places? Our understanding of God is faulty. The way it is presented is often incorrect. We want a God who will meet all our needs as we define them. We decide what our life should be like, and we determine how God should respond to our needs. Yet the biblical emphasis is seen in things like this: Paul tells us that he had learned to be content in every situation, whether well-fed or hungry, in plenty or in want. He is reminding us that we need to live as if God is in control, even though we know that we often want our own way. We long for God to follow our direction.

Why Doesn't God Heal Me?

Isaiah 53:5 tells us that by Jesus' wounds we are healed. But what does that mean? When our first parents sinned, we died spiritually. Jesus' death on the cross bought our eternal salvation, so we are healed from the deadly effects of sin. But what about physical healing?

So here we are, back to John's struggle. Being sick, we want to be well. Our assumption is if God loves us, he also wants us well. But are we seeing the whole plan? Wanting to be like God, we think we know the plan. A quick look at the Scriptures and we are sure—or so we think. By his wounds we are healed. It seems clear enough. But is it? Too often we get it wrong. Job's friends were sure they knew the will of God, and yet they were wrong. Paul prayed for others to be healed, and he assumed God would heal him, too. Jacob met with God, and instead of being healed he walked away a cripple. They all thought they knew, and they all got it wrong.

How, then, are we to know the mind of the Lord? In Romans 12:1-2, Paul tells us to present our bodies as living sacrifices before God, to renew our mind by reading the Word of God, and testing to see what is good and acceptable before God. Knowing God comes by study, prayer, and experience. We know Jesus healed the sick as he walked among them. After the ascension of Jesus, the disciples did acts of healing. God, who is the same yesterday, today, and forever, is still a healing God. But is it a given? We cannot be presumptions about how God will act in any given situation because we do not know what role we are playing in his divine plan. God is in every situation working for our good. What's good for the plan of God might mean my having to face struggles in this present life.

How I understand God determines how I expect him to act. If healing is in the atonement, then when I am sick God must heal me. If he doesn't heal me, then there is something wrong with me. But if God is reconciling the world to himself, then God might be using my condition for a greater good.

God had chosen Joseph to be his instrument to save his family. If God only chose to use those who were worthy, Joseph would be excluded. If God only chose people from intact, trouble-free families, Joseph would not qualify. As we follow the story of Joseph, we will see that he ends up in some pretty dark places. He doesn't seem to be in the will of God. Life goes from bad to worse for him—and yet it is all working out in God's will.

There are not always easy answers to why we find ourselves in the situations that we do. When we quote Scriptures that seem to speak to our situation, we are not always right in our understanding. It would take Joseph years to see what God was doing in his life. What is important, as we walk our spiritual journey, is for us to keep our eyes upon Jesus. We are saved by grace, and nothing can separate us from the love of God. Our self-worth is found in the fact that we bear the image of God. And we walk in confidence that God is in every situation of our lives, working together for our good.

Think about These Things

Take some time to reflect on what you have just read in this chapter, then use the bulleted points below to prayerfully apply these biblical principles to your life and circumstances.

- Something has happened to you. You did not foresee it coming and now you find you are suffering. You know God is sovereign. You read in Scripture that God is love. He could have prevented the situation from happening, but he did not. What does this reveal about God? What does it reveal about you? Given what you have learned, what should you do?
- You may not be able to solve your dilemma, but this you know: it's not your fault. God still cares for you.
- Remember this: your entire theology or even your entire life feels as if it has fallen apart, but God does not fall apart—he is unchanging and, even in this, he will show you that he still cares for you.
- Read and reflect on Romans 8:28.
- Now that you have read this chapter, as you reflect prayerfully on your situation, what is the main challenge you consider you are facing? What one thing can you do today, in light of what you have read in this chapter, can you commit to doing?

2

The Call of God

Steve is a conservative guy. He's thrifty, some say to a fault. He's a hard worker who puts his family future in the forefront of his planning. He holds down a good job and spends his money wisely, making conservative investments.

Savings All Gone!

Thinking the economy to be solid at the time, Steve failed to diversify, placing most of his money in what he thought would be a safe investment. So, when the economy failed in 2007, he woke to the realization that he had lost almost all his savings. Where was God in all of this? He wasn't being foolish; he hadn't thought he was making reckless moves with his money. All he wanted to do was take care of his family and have a secure future for himself and his wife. The family is vitally important in the Scriptures. A husband and father is supposed to care for his family. So, what happened?

Steve was left wrestling with his faith. A lot of things were passing through his mind. Did God not love him? Was that why he found himself in this situation? Did he really trust God—and if so, where was his faith?

Many people believe that if you are a Christian and live right, God will prosper you. Steve's finances went in the opposite direction. Was he even a Christian? Was his real desire to take care of his own life and bypassing his need for God?

Steve wrestled with questions about what others might think of him. What did his family think of him? Would his wife trust his investment planning in the future? What would he say to people who asked how his investments were doing? His pride was hurt. His confidence in his ability to make good business decisions was shaken. More than a decade later, he was was still wrestling with what he viewed as a failure on his part.

Unforseen Crisis Events

Not every crisis is of our own making. We certainly understand when we do wrong and suffer the consequences for our sin. That was not the case in Steve's situation. His actions did not cause the economy to crash. Bad decisions made by large corporations, banks, and investors in the questionable mortgages the banks were selling bought about the recession that ended up causing many families like Steve's to suffer great losses. He and many others suffered for the sin of those they had no relationship with. Sometimes we suffer for other people's sin. It's bad enough when we do wrong and have to answer for it—but can't God deliver us from suffering because of the sins of others?

Habakkuk writes these words:

> Though the fig tree should not blossom,
>   nor fruit be on the vines,
> the produce of the olive fail
>   and the fields yield no food,
> the flock be cut off from the fold
>   and there be no herd in the stalls,
> yet I will rejoice in the LORD;
>   I will take joy in the God of my salvation.
> (Habakkuk 3:17, 18)

The prophet understood that his nation, Israel, was under judgment for its sin and he, as a citizen, would suffer along with everyone else. We live in a fallen society and so when judgment comes, suffering falls upon us all. When the economy went into recession because of the subprime mortgage issue, all the nation suffered. The actions of a few brought calamity on the many. But that is no consolation when we find ourselves in times of struggle. Some struggles are for a time and some for a lifetime, but in either case we cry out, "God, where are you?"

The New Testament tells us this: "And we know that for those who love God all things work together for good, for those who are called according to his purpose" (Romans 8:28). That's a pretty straightforward statement from the apostle Paul, but be sure to note that this is for *those who are called according to his purpose*. So, if God is working for our good, how do we account for the fact that people like Steve lost everything in the recession they had no control over? Why did righteous Habakkuk have to suffer for other people's sins?

Why Suffer because of Other People's Sin?

How may I know whether I have been called according to God's purpose? In the New Testament, a person's assurance of salvation is rooted in the call of God. In John 6:37 Jesus said, "All that the Father gives me will come to me, and whoever comes to me I will never cast out." Verse 40 records how he said, "For this is the will of my Father, that everyone who looks on the Son and believes in him should have eternal life, and I will raise him up on the last day." Salvation begins and ends in God.

From the start and throughout his ministry, Jesus called people to follow him—and that was clearly the will of his Father. People called by God follow him. All his disciples followed him when Jesus called them. The gospel call is always to come and follow Jesus. Those who heed the call are those whom the Father has given to Jesus. We follow and believe through faith—and that faith is a gift from God.

If you are a believer, the assurance of your calling rests not in anything you have done but on God's call, the foundation of your salvation in Jesus. Scripture is clear: whoever believes and is baptized shall be saved (Mark 16:16). Yet, like Steve, you might find yourself in a situation not of your own making—and there are grave consequences. All things do *not* appear to be working for your good.

Following the call of Jesus does not mean we know the path he will take us down. God's plan is often hidden from our eyes. How things are working for our good we do not always grasp or understand. The *how* and *why* are God's doing. What we are responsible to do is follow and obey Jesus, and this we do by faith. We must accept that truth and walk in it. Every time we take our eyes off Jesus and put them on our experiences, we end up in fear and confusion.

Dreamy Joseph

In Genesis 37, we meet Joseph as a seventeen-year-old. He is tending his father's flock with his half-brothers, the sons of Bilhah and Zilpah, and he has brought his father Jacob a bad report of their behavior.

Because Joseph was the favorite son, his brothers hated him and could not even speak kindly to him. They hated his attitude toward them, and they hated the fact that he was more loved by their father. There was nothing in Joseph that caused him to be favored by God.

But Joseph was called by God. Remember that he had had two dreams that made his brothers hate him even more: in one dream the brothers were in a field binding sheaves, and his sheaf stood upright while theirs gathered around it and bowed down to it. Was he to rule over them? In his second dream, the sun, the moon, and eleven stars were bowing down to him. This was enougth for Jacob to rebuke him: "Shall I and your mother and your brothers indeed come to bow ourselves to the ground before you?" The brothers were jealous of him, but Jacob kept the saying in mind. Was there something to this? Was God at work? From his own experience, Jacob knew that God used messed-up people to accomplish his purposes; Joseph was being called by God and being given just a glimpse into what the future would hold for him. He had no idea of the path he was about to follow.

That is how God works. We are given just enough to keep us walking on with the Lord; we are given the big picture, but we live in the here and now. If you are a Christian, it is the hope of glory, the promise of eternal life, the promise of heaven that keeps you going—just as the Nicene Creed declares, "I believe in the resurrection of the dead and the life of the world to come."

We are called to follow Jesus in the journey of life. We don't know the pathway on which we will journey. In the end all things will work out for our good, but it might not seem so in the near future. There will be moments of reprieve when it seems the windows of heaven are opened, and the glory of God is revealed. But often we find ourselves in times of struggle. Our hope is always in the future. God kindly gave Joseph a big-picture glimpse into the future.

Proper Perspective

Suffering financial loss because of the decisions of others is a challenge to our faith, and does not seem to us as if God is working for our good. It raises all kinds of questions. How will I survive in my retirement years? How will my family have to sacrifice because of the situation? Will I be forced to move and downsize?

The Bible repeats to us that the just shall live by faith. We have no guarantees for tomorrow and we are not promised an easy life. We are told that Jesus will never leave us or forsake us, and that God is working for our good. What does that mean in practice?

Our faith struggle comes when we take our eyes off God and his plan, but there are secret plans that he has for us. We are not given the plan in all its fullness. We are only given glimpses and moments of clarity so that we will not lose hope and fall away. Our responsibility is to obey God and follow Jesus wherever he leads, and we are not told to do that for any certain result.

By nature, many of us have a reward-and-punishment mentality. The promise of reward, in whatever we do, pushes us to act correctly. The fear of punishment causes us to refrain from doing evil. So, laws become important for us and our corporate life together and we define life in our nation as characterized by law and order. We assume that life is governed that way. But in real life, things go against our neat-and-tidy view!

Job's Bad Experiences

Think again of the other man in the Old Testament—Job—who went through deep and dark troubles.

Job shines a different light on this discussion. Job's friends believed that if people do good, God will reward them, and if they do evil, God will punish them. They called on Job to repent. His suffering and losses were, they believed, the result of sin in his life. They took a principle that has some merit but they applied it where it did not apply. In reality, Job was in his situation because God was at war with Satan and he, God, was using Job as an example of someone who would not deny him, no matter how bad the situation became. Though it is true God rewards the good and punishes the evil, it is not always evident, so we are left clinging on to God.

Learning from People Like Joseph

God called Joseph and God had a plan for good for him and his family. But things seemed to be falling apart. In the midst of our struggle, what matters to us is getting out of the situation; we want relief. In our shortsightedness, we see only our present situation and not the greater plan of God. We fail to recognize the sovereign purposes of God; we don't see where he is taking us or how we are to get there.

Suffering is part of God's process of making us like Christ. We all have much to learn. God is working on us, conforming us to the image of his Son, Jesus. We may come from different places and have different lessons to learn—just like it was for Steve. Steve's confidence was in his conservative investments and that he wasn't doing anything wrong. Could it be God had a lesson or two for him to learn?

Manna from Heaven?

When the Israelites were leaving Egypt and traveling through the desert, finding food was an issue for such a large body of nomads. They got caught up in their lack of easy, accessible food. Soon they complained to Moses. Moses sought God, and God sent manna each day for them to eat. Just before they entered the Promised Land, Moses recounted all they went through. He reminded them that neither their clothes nor their shoes had become worn out—and then he said something very striking: that God had allowed them to hunger so that they would learn that "man does not live by bread alone, but by every word that comes from the mouth of God" (Deuteronomy 8:3). God allowed them to hunger so they would learn to trust in his divine provision.

There is nothing wrong with planning for the future. In fact, it is the responsible thing to do. But when you plan, you should not say what your intentions are but rather say that if the Lord wills, you will do thus and such (see James 4:13-16). In all you do, be sure to recognize that you are dependent on God. Steve was right to plan, but his future was bound up in Jesus. When Job lost everything, his response glorified God in saying how he, the LORD, *both* gives and takes away.

Looking Ahead

The Bible is not a book of principles and neither is it is a book of rules that, if we follow it, life will go smoothly. No, the Bible is the account of the unfolding of God's loving and redemptive plan for ordinary people like you and me. It starts at the creation and fall, continues through the ministry of Jesus, and it ends with the people of God united around his eternal throne.

The Bible tells us of real people with all their faults as they encounter the living God. There are the different ways God reveals himself to his people Israel, their failure to keep his law, and the opening up of salvation to the Gentiles. In the midst of it all, individual people encounter God. All of this is recorded for our benefit, so that we can learn to trust God, journey toward him, and become conformed to the image of Jesus.

The crisis in Steve's life and the ones in our own are not the important issues. God promises to sustain us and keep us. What is important is that we learn to be like Christ. God holds our future; he gives and takes away. He calls us to be content in every situation. In order to do that, we may well find ourselves in uncomfortable situations. We learn to trust that God will sustain us in our future by having nothing but him to lean upon.

Think about These Things

Take some time to reflect on what you have just read in this chapter, then use the bulleted points below to prayerfully apply these biblical principles to your life and circumstances.

- On a piece of paper, or in a journal, write out your feelings. Perhaps you will say something like this: "The direction of my life is out of control. Other people sinned and affected my future. I'm stuck holding the bag. I made good decisions, but they did not work out."
- Sometimes good and evil seem to be mixed up togther all in one package. It can be difficult to come to terms with this seemingly contradictory juxtaposition. Yet, evil can coexist with God's goodness, even in your pit.
- What kind of feelings does this bring out in you? What parallels do you see in Joseph's story that validate this thinking? Does it encourage you?
- Reflection point: because of God's presence with you, his goodness is not just something with future value; it is present with you right now.
- Even if your life seems to be beyond your control and your plans falter, you can still hold on to God and praise him. Remind yourself of this in words such as these: "I am in the pit, but God is in the pit with me!"
- Read and reflect on Habakkuk 3.
- Now that you have read this chapter, as you reflect prayerfully on your situation, what is the main challenge you consider you are facing? What one thing can you do today, in light of what you have read in this chapter, can you commit to doing?

The Call of God

Section 2:
From Pit to Prison

We have been following Joseph and his difficult relationship with his brothers. The dysfunctional family life has led to hatred and discord among the them. They had no place for their younger sibling. It's at this point Joseph has his dreams about his family, that he will rule over them somehow. He doesn't know the detail of what lies ahead but he does know that, somehow, they will bow before him. This has caused the brothers to be jealous of him. Jealousy is a destructive emotion. They need to somehow remove Joseph so they can get on with their lives.

How often do we allow jealousy to interrupt our lives! Either we become jealous of others or they become jealous of us. When we allow jealousy into our lives we can't move forward. It causes us to sin or be sinned against.

The brothers all move on with their flocks near Shechem. They are all together. Joseph has returned to his father but at one point Jacob sends Joseph to check on them. Remember the last time he brought back a bad report of them? Now he is parading himself in an expensive coat, feeling very entitled. He tracks down his brothers at Dothan—and this is where the family dysfunctionality reaches a head.

The brothers see him approaching them and they decide to put an end to this situation. Perhaps they have been speaking of him in his absence. Their hatred for him had grown to such a level that they decide to kill him and throw his body in a pit and tell their father he has been eaten by a wild animal—then they will see what will become of his dreams!

The dreams have come from God and they give a general overview of what is to take place, but not with the details. The secret things belong to the LORD and the things revealed belong to us so that we can obey the laws of the LORD, something Moses later makes clear in Deuteronomy 29:29. Joseph and his family have no idea what the future holds; they are just given a glimpse of the future, but with no details.

Only Dreams?

The family will have to accept that this is from God. Joseph believed this, though Jacob hides them in his mind, but, for the time being, the brothers have no place for the dreams or the dreamer. They defy God by mocking Joseph and plotting to kill him. If they do away with Joseph, the dreams will be seen as figments of his imagination.

Can you feel the hatred they have for him? When we take our minds off God and his plan, we are left with the future in our own hands. We try to control the future as we define it. We start down a path that takes us away from God. Rejecting the visions as coming from God, the brothers plan to prove *they* are right. But God speaks to the future because he knows it. We cannot, because we do not know, and what the brothers do not understand is that God is in control! Their sinful actions are being incorporated into the plan of God. Plotting to kill Joseph, they know they will have to lie to their father about it. Once we choose to disobey God, other sins will follow.

When Reuben hears of the plan, he convinces them to not kill him, but just to throw him in into a pit. His plan is to rescue Joseph and return him to Jacob.

Joseph has to go through a series of emotions.

First, *fear*. What is going on? Why do his brothers hate him so much and conspire to throw him into this pit? What are their plans for him? Will they leave him here to die? How will he get out?

Then there's the feeling of *rejection*. Surely they are his family? As a self-consumed younger brother, beloved by his father, he has felt he secure in his position. Why were they doing this to him?

Things will go from bad to worse for Joseph. Reuben cannot rescue him. While he is gone, the brothers decide to sell Joseph to some Ishmaelites who, in turn, will sell him into slavery in Egypt. Potiphar purchases Joseph as a house slave. Joseph does right by

Potiphar, and Potiphar puts him in charge of his entire house. All seems well for a time. But Joesph's reprieve doesn't last for long.

Potiphar's wife looks lustfully on Joseph and tries to seduce him. Jospeh keeps rejecting her offers, but one day it comes to a head. She propositions him and again he rejects her overtures, pulling away from her and leaving his clothes in her hands. She is not going to take rejection from a lowly house slave! She runs to Potiphar and accuses Joseph of attempted rape.

Furious, Potiphar throws Joseph into prison. But God is in this. Joseph is incarcertated in the same prison that Pharoah places his prisoners. There, Joseph serves God by doing what is right. The chief prison guard puts Joseph in charge of the prisoners. His life levels out again for a time.

We go through life experiencing many ups and downs. Finding ourselves in difficult situations, we look for the time when things will get better. Everything comes to an end. But there are times when things go from bad to worse. That is Joseph's situation. How are we to act? What are we to do? What does the Lord require of us? In Michah 6:8 we are told what he requires of us:

> He has told you, O man, what is good;
>> and what does the LORD require of you
> but to do justice, and to love kindness,
>> and to walk humbly with your God?

We are to follow God in obedience for no other than that is what God requires of us. We don't work to receive from God; rather, we work to obey him.

3

Did I Really Hear from God?

Faith at Work

Faith is a spiritual exercise. The writer of Hebrews tells us that ". . . faith is the assurance of things hoped for, the conviction of things not seen" (see Hebrews 11:1f). Faith is being sure of what we hope for and convinced that what is not seen is real. The assumption is that God is real and that the things we hope for will come to pass. A lot is riding on this. We live in a world where our understanding is based on what we grasp with our senses. Faith looks beyond our senses and it lays hold of the promises of God. Our struggle is to look past what we see, and to experience the promises of God.

The human experience is a desperate effort to find our self-worth. *Why am I here? What is my purpose in life? Will I be remembered when I am gone? What is the meaning of life?* Our bookstores have rows and rows of self-help books. People are broken, feeling inadequate, and are looking for answers. Plastic surgery is a major industry. Being told by society that they are not pretty enough, people spend thousands of dollars to "fix" their looks. Credit debt has skyrocketed as people live beyond their means, all in an effort to impress those around them. When we turn from God, we are left on our own to figure out our worth as human beings and the value of our lives on this planet.

The fall has taken its toll on all of us. Not only is there a desperate attempt to find self-worth in what we do, but there is another effect. If we can't find our worth in what we do, competition is stiff, so we tend to put others down. No one wants to own up to his or her shortcomings, so the tendency is to blame others. When Eve was caught trying to be like God, she blamed the devil. Adam, on the other hand, blamed God for giving him such a weak woman. So, as we strive to improve ourselves, we push others down in the process. This is all to make ourselves feel needed and important.

We must ask ourselves questions like these: What is the foundation of our actions? What is our worldview—the theological belief (our view of what God is like)—that is the basis of our actions? There is a war, the apostle Paul tells us, in our inner lives, a pull to either do what pleasing to God or what is according to the values of this present world. If we do not think about it, the world will pull us away from God. It has been our condition since the fall. We want control of our circumstances; we want to be the god of our lives. But the Holy Spirit is active in the lives of believers. He actively calls us to follow Christ. As we read the Word of God, the Spirit speaks to us revealing the will of God to us. This is the reason for Paul's inner struggle, which is the struggle of every believer—the pull of the Spirit to do what is right, and the pull of the flesh to satisfy its own desires. The Christian life is one of service. We are called to love God and our neighbor.

The world tells us to put ourselves first. We seek creaturely comforts. We look for a smooth and easy life. Success is viewed as prosperity and health. The goal is to rule rather than to serve. Service is seen as something extra that we do, not the purpose of our life. When the Holy Spirit enters us, our worldview is challenged, and the internal struggle begins. It's in the clash of these two worldviews that our Christian growth takes place.

Our tendency is to go through life unquestioningly. We try to follow God as best we can. We attend church, pray, read our Bibles and contribute what we can to the work of the church. We face the normal ups and downs of life, taking them in our stride.

Reasons Why Joseph May Have Doubted

Joseph believed in God; his father, Jacob, had encountered God many times. He was raised to believe in and serve God. He didn't have the Scriptures—they were yet to be written—but he knew and served God despite the confusion of his family situation. He went through life as most of us do, believing in God and walking through life trusting that all was well. At one point, he had a series of visions from God. Hearing from God gave his life purpose and direction. He was so sure he heard from God, he told his family what God had spoken to him. We have the Scriptures, the Word of God. We hear from God as we read the Bible, and the Spirit of God speaks to us and applies its words to our lives. We walk in the confidence that God speaks to us, and we know his will. Most of the time we rest in the love of God.

In spite of all that Joseph went through with his brothers, he felt secure in his position. His father loved and protected him from the feelings his brothers had toward him. He had no fear of them. So, when his brothers had finally had enough of the dreamer, they planned his demise. On one of his visits to them in the pastures, they grabbed him and threw him into a pit. It was there that life in all its harshness confronted Joseph. It was in the pit that his faith rubbed up against the reality of life. What was happening to him? Had he really heard from God or was it all in his head? Was his imagination running wild or had God really said. . . ?

When we walk with God, there are times when we might find ourselves in a pit. The pit is that place where the problems of life confront us—when our faith comes up against what is seemingly impossible. The promises of God seem unreal. Did God actually say those things? It's a dark and discouraging place. One's confidence falters and faith is on the line.

Mary's Story

Mary grew up attending church. She always professed faith in Christ. She was not a very strong Christian; she didn't pray much but believed that God would always take care of her. She migrated to America, got married, and had children. This sent her back to church on a regular basis.

Reality kicked in when she received news that it was very likely she would face kidney failure. She kind of trusted God, believing he would not let it happen to her. When the possibility became reality, she found herself in a pit. Her initial reaction was that God was punishing her for something she had done wrong. She had little hope that she would receive a transplant and viewed her diagnosis as a death sentence. It can get very dark in the pit.

When you find yourself in a pit, it seems like there is no way out. You find yourself there because of circumstances beyond your control and there is nothing you can do to free yourself from it. When you find yourself in situations where you have no control, all you are left with is God. When times are good, that's easy to say, and it's comforting, too. But in the pit it's different! Feelings of fear, doubt, and discouragement become overwhelming. That easy assurance one has when all is going well is challenged in the pit. *Where is God? What did I do wrong to deserve this? Is God real? Did he really say. . . ?* All of the promises of God are challenged.

Joseph had no explanation for his condition. He knew his brothers didn't like him, but this was pushing things too far. What was going to happen to him? Would they kill him? He heard them talking. Would they just leave him to die a slow death? How horrible!

We're not told how long Joseph remained there. For some people, the pit is short term—perhaps a few days. But for others, it can last years. Mary waited six years to hear these words: "We've located a donor!"

At one point, Joseph heard his brothers talking but he couldn't make out what they were saying. Then something extraordinary happened: They threw a rope down and told him to take hold of it. They were going to pull him out. Was this just a gag, a bad joke on their part? He knew they didn't like him but for the sake of their father maybe they had experienced a change of heart. Sometimes a ray of light shines in the pit and there is a bit of hope.

Mary dropped what she was doing and rushed to the hospital. Time was of the essence. God was in control; he was going to make this all right. In a fresh burst of hope, faith sprang to life in her. By the time she was checked in and was ready to proceed with the operation, word came to her that the kidney was damaged and could not be used. The second pit was worse than the first. Was God teasing her? This just seemed cruel.

They dragged Joseph out of the pit and bound him with rope. There was a band of Ishmaelites passing by. The brothers sold Joseph to them, and they carried him off to Egypt. There he was sold as a slave to Potiphar, a commander in the company of Egypt.

Struggling but Winning

Our struggle revolves around our expectations of what we assume God should or would do. If we are expecting God to give us a free and easy life, we are thrown when things go bad. How we view our life experiences will determine how we approach life. If we are expecting God to make our life easy all the time, we will be disappointed.

As a young Christian I was told if you give your life to Jesus, all your needs would be met and all your problems would be solved. Over time I have learned that Christians face the same life struggles as everyone else. Life is filled with pits. There is really no way to avoid them. So, what gets us through those times of struggle and doubt?

The story of Abraham and Isaac teaches us that God's time is not our time. We live in an age of immediate gratification. We don't want to wait for anything. We want the world, and we want it now. We order online and want same-day or at least next-day order delivery. So, when we end up in a pit, we want to pray and then experience immediate deliverance. When we don't get it, we think it must be our fault. Our theology tells us God wants to deliver us as soon as we seek his face in prayer. Or if we are sick, we must be healed immediately. If this doesn't take place, we are at fault, we are told, and we find ourselves wondering what we did that was wrong.

Our faith rests on the fact that God exists and has sent Jesus to redeem us. Jesus is the evidence of God's love for us. If he did not spare his Son to save us, surely he will withhold no good thing from us. That is what he has told us—and our faith rests on the promises of God to us. Our trust is in Jesus our Savior, and our hope is in the resurrection of the dead and the life of the world to come. God has promised that those who believe in Jesus will inherit eternal life. God's promises are sure. They are just as sure as when God spoke to Joseph in a dream that his family would bow before him.

When we find ourselves in the pit, we need to press ourselves into the promises of God, for they never change. Nothing changed in God's mind or his plans to deliver Jacob's family when the brothers threw Joseph into the pit. God wasn't caught by surprise. It wasn't as if he didn't see it coming. Likewise, Mary's failed kidney didn't change God's love toward her. Too often we think these kinds of situations do change God's love toward us. Either we have done something wrong and God is punishing us, or he has no control of the situation; neither one of those options is satisfactory.

When you find yourself in a pit, you need to return to the Word of God. What did he say? What was his promise to me? Our minds want answers. We want to find some rational explanation for what we are going through. It seems unsatisfactory to simply say that God is in control. We want more. Like little children, we ask why. Sometimes there will be no answer. Job longed to make his case before God, for he, too, wanted some answers. In the end God told him to just be quiet and to trust in his mercy.

God Has Redeeming Purposes

God was moving his redemptive plan forward and Joseph was an integral part of that plan. God had revealed that to him in the two dreams he received. It would eventually make sense to him—but not yet. Joseph had to learn some things about himself and God before he could lead his family out of their struggles.

A famine was coming, and Joseph was going to be used by God to deliver the family, but there was no way at this point that he could understand what God was doing. At the time the brothers threw him in the pit, there was no famine. Life was good for Jacob and his family. They were prospering and everything was fine. They had no way of knowing what lay ahead for them.

So much in this story was unknown to the people involved at the time. They did not know that in a few years they would be living through a famine that could destroy them. But even they should have known that the promise to Abraham was still in effect. They, too, had the promise of God to lean upon. Joseph had his dreams. They had the promise to Abraham.

Our human response is often one of reaction. We react to the situations we find ourselves in. Something happens, and we try to figure out our next move. Our default mode is to try to reasonably understand what is happening to us. Somehow the unknown disturbs us. We are uncomfortable not having a reason for our situation. So, we grab at straws. We cannot sit with unresolved conflict in our life. There has to be a reason for the situations we find ourselves in. Our mind cannot rest with uncertainty.

There was a reason Joseph was in the pit. Some of it he could understand but the real reason was beyond his grasp. He was there on one level because of the conflict with his brothers. It was inexcusable behavior on their part, but it was understandable. The mental dilemma for Joseph was this: what about the dreams? He could trust his understanding of the situation and try to address the family's dysfunctional nature and why his brothers' hatred of him had led them to do what they did, but to do that he would have to disregard the dreams. And if he did that, in light of his present situation, the dreams semingly could not have been from God. Or if he held on to the dreams, he was left trying to understand the situation he found himself in. I believe at the time he was left with no simple answer. He had heard from God, and he needed to hold on to that in spite of all he was now going through. To do otherwise would have left him in a world without God and without hope.

A world without God is a world in chaos—a world with no rational explanation for anything that happens. Life would be a series of chance happenings. One would move through life reacting to situations as they happen with no goal and reason for the events that take place. If we believe that God exists, we must believe that he is in control of all things, he is sovereign, and that he is moving us to his appointed goal which he has revealed to us—the final redemption of his creation. For Christians, our hope is in the resurrection of the dead and the life of the world to come. We believe God has spoken to us in his Word and his promise of eternal life is sure.

Life is full of pits. We will, at times, fall into them. We must remind ourselves that God has spoken and that his Word to us is sure. At the end of the age or at the end of our life on this planet, we will stand before him. When we find ourselves in a pit, we will and we should ask questions. How did we end up here?

There are life lessons to be learned, but we will never

understand all of the reasons we land in pits. God is working on us, conforming us to the image of his Son, Jesus, but there is a bigger picture. It is the redemptive plan of God. What role are we playing in that? God often keeps that a secret from us.

Like Joseph, you have some issues to deal with that put you in a pit, but God has bigger plans for you in his redemptive story.

Think about These Things

Take some time to reflect on what you have just read in this chapter, then use the bulleted points below to prayerfully apply these biblical principles to your life and circumstances.

- On a piece of paper, or in a journal, write out your feelings. Perhaps you will say something like this: "I'm really wrestling with the way I am feeling so sick—seriously sick—and I feel like I am suffering and there is nobody to blame. I am only left with questions. Why is this happening to me?"
- Sometimes sin and the effects of sin are not the result of bad decisions alone, but are the result of living in a fallen world. It's the very nature of our existence. As a Christian, you do not have immunity from suffering. Therefore, Jesus understands. His redeeming work will make all things right, but for the moment you need to cast your cares on him for he cares for you.
- When you read about Joseph and reflect on your own pit, are you prone to doubt God's care for you?
- Read and reflect on 1 Peter 5 and Psalm 55.
- Now that you have read this chapter, as you reflect prayerfully on your situation, what is the main challenge you consider you are facing? What one thing can you do today, in light of what you have read in this chapter, can you commit to doing?

4

How Did I End up in This Pit?

How Did It Happen?

The question remains: How did I end up in this pit? We have looked at what to think about what it means to be in the pit, realizing that God uses those experiences for his own will and purpose. We have come to understand that there is spiritual growth for the person in the pit. God is using every situation in our lives to conform us into the image of Jesus. This helps us in our faith walk to see the hand of God in what we are going through. God is in every situation working for the good of those who are called according to his purposes. We understand that God is in the process of reconciling the world to himself. All this is helpful for us to understand what God is doing while we are in the pit. But the question I hear from many people is this: How did I get here? What caused me to be in this situation?

We are not fatalists. Scripture does not tell us that God moves us like chess pieces across the world. We are not just along for the ride. God gave Adam and Eve a command, and with it a choice. They were commanded not to eat of the fruit of the Tree of the Knowledge of Good and Evil. The day they did they would die. The command was that they were not to eat. The choice to obey was theirs—obey and live; disobey and die. Our decisions matter, but they matter as they are worked into the eternal mind of God. Nothing happens outside the will and purposes of God.

This is illustrated in what Paul has wrtten: "Therefore, my beloved, as you have obeyed, so now, not only as in my presence but much more in my absence, work out your own salvation with fear and trembling for it is God who works in you, both to will and to work his good pleasure" (Philippians 2:12-13). As we make our life decisions, it is God behind the scenes working his will and good pleasure.

We live in a world where much is beyond our control. This world is fallen. When our first parents sinned, all of creation suffered. The ground no longer yielded to the hand of man but fought against him. We now have to engage in wearisome toil for our existence. Sin has affected every part of our life on this planet. Sickness and death plague our mortal existence. War and conflict are a daily experience. The fall separated us from God, when we were driven from his presence, but also our relationships with other people have also been broken. The reality of the fall needs to factor in the way we think about our life and where we end up.

So far, we have looked at three individuals: John, Steve, and Mary. Each of them found himself or herself in a deep pit. Each was overcome by the surrounding circumstances and had to wrestle with God's will and purpose. Each of them had little control over what had happened and had to come to the place of receiving from the Lord whatever he had in store. The hymn writer states it so clearly: "What e'er my God ordains is right." This is more easily said than experienced but nevertheless true. Yet the question remains in our mind: How did I get into this pit?

When Bad Things Happen

John was a safe and experienced hunter. He hunted not only for sport but also for survival. He made a hasty decision that led to his fall. But accidents happen—most of the time without consequences. But that time it had lasting effects. God didn't protect him. He allowed him to fall. God always remains in control. Satan could take everything from Job, including his health. He just could not take his life, for God set the parameters. He remained in control. Satan did his deeds but God determined what he would allow to happen. For numerous reasons we have discussed, God let John fall. This seems like a harsh reality, and if God had no purpose, the fall would be in vain.

Steve made what he thought were good and safe investments for his and his family's future. In hindsight he would have done things differently, but hindsight is always 20/20. He did nothing wrong, but the economy crashed and he became a victim of other peoples' sin. He was in a pit—but it was not one of his own making.

Mary got sick. It wasn't the result of a bad lifestyle; it was genetic, the result of the effects of the fall on all humankind. She, too, was in a pit—one not of her own making or the making of other peoples' sin. She was in the pit because she lives in a fallen world.

Joseph

Joseph was in the pit because his brothers didn't like what he said and they didn't believe he had heard from God. They sought to do away with the dreamer. They rejected the idea that the dreams that Joseph had were from God. If they could just do away with Joseph, they would do away with the dreams. Then what God revealed to Joseph—that his family would bow down to him—could not come to pass. They were, in effect, trying to put an end to the plan of God. They did not understand what they were trying to do because they did not believe, for whatever reason, that the dreams had come from God. They were responding emotionally to the perceived arrogance of the brother they hated.

We live casuistically—that is, we move through life acting on events that we find ourselves in, waiting for a reaction and then responding again with little or no thought for the overall plan of God. Joseph's family was dysfunctional; the brothers did not get along, so when Joseph had a dream that they interpreted as him placing himself above them, they were enraged. They never questioned if the dreams were from God. Rather, they just reacted emotionally to the situation. They did not seek God about the matter. They could not see the overall plan of God, even though God had given them enough information to trust him for they had the promise to Abraham.

The brothers acted in response to the situation they found themselves in, with no idea what lay ahead. They did not foresee the famine that would take place a decade or more in the future. They had no idea of how it would affect the survival of their family. Joseph's dream was actually a picture of God's plan of salvation for them, but in their anger, they missed it.

Looking back on the event, we become aware of the unseen hand of God. This family had been chosen by God to represent him to the world. They would be the nation of Israel. There was going to be a seven-year period of prosperity followed by seven years of famine. God was raising up Joseph to orchestrate the plan that would save both Egypt and the family of Jacob and move the promise of Abraham forward.

In order to do that, Joseph would have to go through years of suffering. One man would have to suffer for the good of the nation. We understand that when we think of the life and ministry of Jesus who made the ultimate sacrifice, but the same principle also has application in the lives of others used by God.

We know from Scripture that life comes out of death. Jesus dies for the sins of the world, rises from the dead, and gives life to all who believe in him. Jesus applies that same truth to us. Unless a grain of wheat falls to the ground and dies, it will not bear fruit (see John 12:24-26). He who keeps his life shall lose it but he who loses his life for Christ and the kingdom will find it (see Matthew 16:25). Jesus tells us to take up our cross daily and follow him. Life comes from death. Joseph will have to die to his life so that his family may live. Things will never be the same. Joseph will never go back to the life he knew in his family. He will establish them in Goshen but he will live in the courts of Egypt. God uses events to change the trajectory of our lives.

So let's get back to this question: How did I get into this pit? We are all moving on a path toward a God-ordained plan for us. "For those whom he foreknew he also predestined to be conformed to the image of his Son. . ." (see Romans 8:28f). Behind all that takes place in our lives is the invisible hand of God ordering our steps to accomplish his will for us. He is working to accomplish his will and purposes. We are not always aware of all that God is doing. We are living experience by experience and are often caught by surprise when things do not work out as we expect them to. So, when we find ourself in a crisis, we ask how we ended up in such a pit. It ultimately falls back on the plan of God for our lives. In the complex world we live in, God is working on us and he is moving his redemptive plan forward. The immediate circumstances for us may look arbitrary and, at times, unfair. "What did I do to deserve this?" we find ourselves asking.

Our choices and decisions determine where we end up. They help create the situations we find ourselves in. Our decisions place us in various situations and at times we are overwhelmed. Life and faith collide, and we find ourselves in a pit. John failed to strap himself in properly, and accidents happen. Steve took a chance on a safe bet and lost. They found themselves in terrible situations.

Seen and Unseen

What our conscious mind wants is an answer. "I am in this situation because. . ." This desire for answers is the reason so many people fall for conspiracy theories. The mind is not content with uncertainty. It searches for reasons for the situations we find ourselves in. Here is where faith comes to give us sound direction There is always a reason for what we are going through, only often it is hidden from us. Life takes place on many levels. There is the seen world in which we experience life, but there is also the unseen spiritual world.

As Christians, we start with the presupposition that God is present, and that behind the world we see and experience is the mystical hand of God ordering life and moving us to a preordained end. This does not minimize or trivialize our decisions but it adds meaning and purpose to our life. We understand that behind what can be seen is the invisible hand of God working out his purposes. Yet in this, our conscious mind moves us through life. We plan ahead and we make decisions. As Christians, we seek to apply the Word of God to the way we live our lives.

There is another perspective also taking place in our lives. We are the products of our culture. We grew up in a certain family, in a certain place, among a certain group of people, and we have a certain ancestral past. All of these influences contribute to who we are. Even the church we attend affects how we view and move through the world. No matter how much we try, our culture affects how we understand God and his actions in our life. This is unavoidable and so, like the apostle Paul, we find that we only see through a glass dimly. This is unavoidable. We are finite individuals trying to comprehend the movement of an infinite God. We are also fallen creatures living in a fallen world. As mentioned earlier, Martin Luther is clearly right when he calls us sinner-saints. Even people who are redeemed do not see the movement of God clearly. The purpose of God's redemptive work is the unfolding plan to unite fallen creation back to him. We can only know God because he reveals himself to us. Otherwise, he remains incomprehensible to us.

Knowing God

God reveals himself to us in many ways. In Romans 1, Paul tells us the he reveals himself to all mankind in creation, leaving us without excuse about an awareness of God. He more clearly reveals himself in his Word. The Holy Spirit speaks to us through the writings of the prophets and the writers of Scripture. Ultimately, God most clearly reveals himself to us in Jesus Christ. God took on flesh and lived among us. When we see Jesus, we see the Father. We live 2,000 years after the coming of Jesus. We add to all of this the history of the church. The writings of the church Fathers, the many creeds of the church, and many teachers have been used by God to speak to us and reveal himself to us. But our relationship to God is ultimately a personal one. It is not just or primarily about information. God wants us to know him and be transformed into the image of Jesus. ". . . we shall be like him, because we shall see him as he is," John tells us in 1 John 3:2.

So, let's go back to the question: How did I get into this pit? God reveals himself to us in our struggles. Paul said he wanted to know Christ in his sufferings. At the end of his ordeal, Job could say, "My ears had heard of you, but now my eyes have seen you" (see Job 42:5). Faith becomes real when we find ourselves in a pit. Joseph knew of God though his father Jacob. He received two dreams from God and he believed they were from God. But he didn't know God in an intimate way until the end of his trials.

In the New Testament, James tells us to count it all joy when we face many trials and temptations because God is working on our character (see James 1:2-4). He is teaching us to trust him and strengthen our faith. Faith is laying hold of the unseen. We end up in pits for a number of reasons but the assurance we have is that God is in there with us, working circumstances together for our good and accomplishing his purposes in our life and for the good of his creation.

The original sin—the sin of our first parents—was the desire to be like God. Our frustration comes when we realize we are not in control of our lives. There is very little in our lives that we have any real control over, yet our desire is to be like God. We don't always admit that to ourselves. It's the reason so many people avoid real prayer until a crisis comes. When we are in a pit, we are suddenly aware that we are not in control, and we need to call upon the Lord. That's a process of conforming to Jesus. "The trying of your faith produces steadfastness. And let steadfastness have its full effect, that you may be perfect and complete, lacking in nothing," James continues (James 1:2-4). We need to learn to come to terms with the pits we fall into because our loving heavenly Father is working on us. That is the part of our walk with God where we gain experience in life. We are learning to trust him, and he is revealing himself to us.

The unseen part, which is of greater importance, is that we are part of a bigger plan. This is why not all pit experiences end on a positive note in this life. Some people are called to be martyrs. Joseph comes out of the pit and ends up in Pharoah's court, second only to him in Egyptian power—a happy ending to a long and difficult trial.

For Paul, it was another story. Paul, too, was told by God he would take the gospel to the highest officials in the Roman Empire. He would stand before Caesar. Paul, like Joseph, was arrested and thrown into prison. But unlike Joseph, Paul did not get out. As a Roman citizen, Paul appealed to Caesar and the Jewish leaders had to send him to Roma. They could not try him themselves so Paul got to state his case in the courts of Rome, but tradition tells us he was never released and died as a martyr.

Joseph's role in the plan of God was to save his family and move the promise to Abraham forward. Paul's role was to take the gospel message to the high courts of the most powerful nation at the time where the gospel woiuld eventually flourish.

God used both of these men in his ultimate plan of redemption.

One enjoyed blessing in this life, and the other entered into the presence of God, leaving this life behind.

God is using each one of us in his redemptive plan. God could speak a word from heaven and save the world, but he has chosen the foolish things of this world to confound the wise. We are God's hands and mouthpiece to take to gospel to a lost and dying world. What we go through, and how we respond, is one way God speaks to the people around us. How we end up in the pit is not as important as what we do when we are there.

Think about These Things

Take some time to reflect on what you have just read in this chapter, then use the bulleted points below to prayerfully apply these biblical principles to your life and circumstances.

- On a piece of paper, or in a journal, write out your feelings. Perhaps you will say something like this: "My decisions matter and I realize that choices bring consequences. But choices really only matter when they are incorporated within the plan of God. I am in my pit because God is accomplishing his purposes in my life. Beyond these purposes, there is a route for me, like Joseph, to reach Pharaoh. Just as with the apostle Paul, it may be my destiny is to reach Caesar, notwithstanding alll the attendant risks—and who knows what this could mean for Caesar's empire, the world, as the knowledge of God through Christ might reach people in far-flung places? Sometimes tragedies happen now, but God will triumph later."
- Are you prepared to be in the pit for the time being, knowing God is with you and wisely, lovingly, working out all things for your long-term good?
- Will you commit to doing the right thing, no matter what? It may put you on a track to meet just the right person or to encounter a new and life-changing situation.
- Reflect on this: You are not forgotten by God. The plan of God is still at work. His will will never be overruled!
- Read and reflect on Job 1.
- Now that you have read this chapter, as you reflect prayerfully on your situation, what is the main challenge you consider you are facing? What one thing can you do today, in light of what you have read in this chapter, can you commit to doing?

5

*From
Bad to Worse*

The pit is not a onetime experience. Living in this fallen world, we often find we move from one bad situation to another. That was Sharon's experience.

Sharon's Trials

Sharon had a series of life-threatening health issues, and recently they had gotten worse. Two years earlier, she had a heart attack that required a quadruple bypass. This was a very serious operation that is not always successful. At age sixty-five, for her the mortality issues were a real consideration. Would she make it through or was this the time that God would take her home? She endured a successful operation. But now, two years later when she was finally feeling she had recovered, a second hammer blow fell—she found she had breast cancer. One experience of facing death is difficult to deal with but another one within two years really pushed the envelope. She was sure that this could be the end. She entered into a dark pit in her walk with the Lord. Why was this happening?

When situations pile up like this, there seems to be no way out. You climb out of one pit, as difficult as it may have been, you take a deep breath, and you move on. Everyone goes through hard times. But when they start to pile up, it's an entirely different matter. How much can one person take? How can one continue to bounce back?

Our minds seek answers and resolutions to unexplained situations. Dealing with one experience is hard enough but when one is forced to move from one pit to another it becomes more difficult. Sharon found herself down in a dark hole. All her fears came rushing back. Fears, regrets, and struggles rushed upon her. Life was fleeting and she had no control. What was God doing?

Joseph was pulled out of the pit by his brothers. Any idea that this was the end of his trial was short-lived. He was sold to a traveling band of Ishmaelites who dragged him to Egypt and sold him to Potiphar. When you're in the pit, all you can do is obey God to the best of your ability—even or especially if you have no idea of what's going on and everything seems out of control. Joseph set out to serve his master as best he could—as unto the Lord. He didn't resist. He accepted his situation and walked with the Lord. Potiphar was pleased and gave Joesph responsibility over his whole house. God blessed Joseph; and Potiphar prospered because of it.

Learning the "New Normal"

When you find yourself in a situation you have no control over—a pit—all you can do is obey the Lord. When he was asked what the greatest commandment was, Jesus stated that it was to love God with your whole being and love your neighbor as you love yourself (see Mark 12:30-31). We are told in Scripture that other people will know we are Christians by our love (see John 13:35). So, when you are stuck in situations beyond your control, you should serve God by doing the right thing—not for reward but simply because it is the right thing to do. In the house of Potiphar where he was a slave, Joseph did not rebel; rather, he served Potiphar as unto the Lord. Joseph was trusted and Potiphar prospered. Joseph settled into a kind of "new normal."

After her surgery and a long recovery, Sharon began to function again as she walked with the Lord. After a difficult situation, things never go back to the way they were. We find ourselves changed by such circumstances. Joseph could not return to his family. He had to learn to live in his "new normal." Situations and experiences change us.

Joseph's "new normal" would not last for long. Potiphar's wife took a liking to him. She continued to make passes at Joseph. One day, things got out of control. She approached Joseph and, as usual, he refused to be lured by her. She pressed in, and he turned to run away. As he did, she grabbed his tunic and it came off in her hand. Not to be a woman scorned, she ran to her husband with Joseph's tunic in hand and accused him of attempted rape. In a just world, Joseph would have had an opportunity to defend himself but he was a slave—and Potiphar sided with his wife. Joseph was sent to prison.

There is the world as it should be, and there is the world as it is. We long to live in the world as it should be. We want to live in a world that is fair. But this world is fallen. Many times, we find ourselves in situations that are just not fair, and we suffer for it. Joseph, in spite of the situation he found himself in, was seeking to do the right thing. He worked hard and honorably for Potiphar. He had a good track record. He should have been given the benefit of the doubt when he was falsely accused, but he wasn't. Life is not fair.

When we land in a pit, the "why" question is right on our lips. "Why is this happening to me?" It's the question on the lips of Job throughout his story. We ask it all the time: "Why is this happening to me?" I am sure it was on Joseph's mind when his brothers threw him into the pit, when they sold him to the Ishmaelites, and when he was taken to Egypt and sold to Potiphar. Things were now getting even worse. Not only was he a slave in a foreign land; he was now a prisoner in that land.

What did Joseph do when he found himself in prison? He did what he did in Potiphar's house: he became an exemplary prisoner. Whatever situation we find ourselves in our response has to be to serve the Lord to the best of our ability. We often balk at that idea. The situation we are in is deemed as not fair. Doubt, fear, and anger are natural responses we feel in our flesh. Job questioned God, and God did not punish him for it. Yet such responses are not responses of faith, and as Christians we should walk by faith and not by sight. For all the reasons we might be in the pit, learning to trust and follow God is certainly one of them.

I have been making the point that behind the seen world is the unseen world of the movement of God. It is God who allows or leads us into the pit. The Spirit of God led Jesus into the wilderness to be tempted by the devil. God controls our lives and orders our steps according to his divine will and purpose. That being the case, we need to acknowledge Jesus in the pit with us. Remember, God is in every situation working for our good. We are never outside the will of God for our lives. This doesn't mean that every situation is good, or comfortable; but it does mean that God has a purpose for us being there. Therefore, our best response in every situation is to serve the Lord.

Joseph was right to do his best for Potiphar because God was with him and he was serving him—God, not Potiphar. In prison, it was the same. As bad as it got, God was still with him and so, as he knew God's presence, he needed to do the best that he could in that horrible environment.

Good Times, Bad Times

We are called to follow Jesus. As Christians, we are not walking aimlessly through life. The call of Jesus is always to follow him. We do not necessarily know where we are going day by day, and we have not been given a road map! We are just told to follow him. When life is good, when there are few obstacles, when people are treating us nicely, and when our health is good, we are glad to follow Jesus. We might even think that our pleasant situation is because of the blessing of God—and it is. But being in the pit doesn't change that. In the pit where he was a slave, and in prison, Joseph was still in the presence of God, and God was leading him to his appointed end.

It means little to serve God only in the good times. It's not really obedience when you are doing what you love to do and when you would do it even if you weren't asked. Obedience matters when you are doing something you would rather not have to do. Even Jesus tells us that loving our friends and those who love us back is not an honorable thing. The act of obedience to the command of God is to love our enemies and do good to those who seek to do us harm (see Matthew 5:44-45). So, the challenge before us is how to act when we are thrown into a pit and what to do when things go from bad to worse.

God was going to ask Joseph to forgive and serve. As a slave in Egypt, he had lost all of his rights and had to serve a foreign dignitary. Then he ended up in a foreign prison. What could God possibly require of him? The prophet Micah, if he had been alive in those days, would likely have told him to do justice, love kindness, walk humbly before God (see Michah 6:8). God expected Joseph to love him and to love his neighbor, even if his neighbor was his master or his prison guard.

Our circumstances do not have to dictate our actions. We are to love and follow Jesus wherever he leads us. Paul also found himself in prison (see Acts 16). God sent an earthquake that shook the gate open. Paul could have fled, which would have led to the punishment of the prison guard. Instead, he remained in his cell and told the guard not to harm himself. God used the situation to lead the guard to faith in Jesus. We are not in control of the situations we find ourselves in. God uses them for his purposes.

Pain and Trauma

Knowing how to respond to God while in the pit does not necessarily ease the pain and trauma you experience there. In Joseph's case, the decline continued. He was not like any others who were in prison there, and he had not had a trial before his peers. Potiphar simply had him arrested and thrown into jail. What was the sentence? We are not told if there even was one. For all we know, his time there was to be indefinite. How discouraging for Joseph! But even when we are in a pit, there are moments of encouragement. Joseph had found favor with the jailer and then something happened to show that God was on the scene again.

At a certain point, two new prisoners arrived—the baker and cupbearer of Pharoah. We are not told what they had done but it angered Pharoah enough that he had them thrown in prison, and there they met up with Joseph. They were placed under his care. They were there for some time. One night they each had a dream which troubled them. In the morning, Joseph discerned that they were troubled and he asked them what the matter was. They told him they each had an unsettling dream that no one could interpret for them. Joseph, still holding tenaciously to God, asked to hear their dreams.

The cupbearer had seen a vine with three branches. As soon as they budded, they ripened into grapes and the king's cup he held in his hand filled with wine which he gave to Pharoah. God intervened and gave Joseph the interpretation; in three days the cupbearer would be restored to his position. Joseph urged him with these words:, "Only remember me, when it is well with you, and please do me the kindness to mention me to Pharoah, and so get me out of this house. For I was indeed stolen out of the land of the Hebrews, and here also I have done nothing that they should put me into the pit." (See Genesis 40:14.)

The baker did not fare as well. He dreamt that he had a basket on his head filled with three cakes for Pharoah. Birds came and ate the contents of the basket. Joseph was again given the interpretation of the dream. In three days, the baker would be put to death. In both cases, Joseph was given the interpretation by God.

This is the second time that God used dreams to assure Joseph that he was with him. The first time involved the dreams he gave him way back before his trials started. Now God had met him in prison and used the dreams of the baker and cupbearer to assure Joseph he was with him in his prison cell. There are moments when we are in a pit where God will make himself known to us, assuring us of his presence, reminding us he is in the situation working for our good.

Joseph reveals a lot in his response to the cupbearer. He remembers the injustice of his situation. He had been stolen from his homeland and had been in prison for no reason and identifies it as a pit. Yet in spite of the despair, there is a glimmer of hope. In effect he was saying, "Remember me when you get out and mention me to Pharoah. Maybe because of your position he will free me."

The plan of God is beginning to unfold for us as we read this account. Pharoah is the goal. God gives us insight in what lies ahead for Joseph. But just as with the first dreams, he gets something to hang on to but he doesn't quite get the plan. Here he realizes God is with him and he has a bit of hope that his trial could end. Sometimes in the midst of our struggle, we sense the presence of God. It is important to remember that Jesus promised to never leave us or forsake us and that he is with us always. God doesn't have to come to visit us in the pit; he is already in the pit with us at all times.

Three days after Joseph interpreted the dreams, the baker

was taken out and executed and the cupbearer was restored to Pharoah. God had revealed himself to Joseph by revealing the meaning of the dreams to him. Joseph must have been encouraged by this. In spite of all the injustice he was experiencing, God was still with him. God was making a way out for him. The cupbearer would plead his case for him before Pharoah and he would soon be out.

Dealing with Ongoing Disappointment

Those moments of encouragement help to sustain us through our time in the pit. It had been an up-and-down journey for Joseph; he had been thrown in the pit by his brothers but pulled out only to be sold into slavery. He had found favor with Potiphar only to be falsely accused by his wife and thrown into prison. He had found favor with the prison guard and now it was beginning to look like he would finally come to the end of this mess that had been going on for many years. But then we read, "The chief cupbearer did not remember Joseph, but forgot him." Joseph would remain in prison for some time yet. He was not coming out of the pit just then! You can only imagine the discouragement he must have felt. Perhaps for the first week or two he could hold on to the hope that he was not forgotten, but as time went on and he began to realize that he was not getting out—that he had been forgotten—a deeper darkness set in. Again, he had been used by God for the good of others, but his situation continued to decline.

Just because God assures us in the pit that he is with us does not mean that the pit experience is coming to an end. There is a greater plan that is being unfolded. In Joseph's case, God was revealing it. He was giving Joseph something to hang on to as he does for us when we look into his Word. He would get to Pharoah—but just not yet. Timing is our problem. A day for the Lord is like a thousand years and a thousand years is like a day (see 2 Peter 3:8). God was moving Joseph along at his appointed time. He was making himself known to Joseph throughout his trial so he would not lose hope. Joseph needed to trust and hang on. We call that faith. Joseph may have had his own time schedule, but it was not God's.

When we go through struggles and find ourselves in a pit, the important thing is to hang on to God. Job raises the question for us: "Shall I receive good from God, and shall I not receive evil?" (see Job 2:10). Sometimes we come out of the pit and are restored. Other times God has a different plan for us. What is important is that we hold on to God. Our goal is the resurrection of the dead and the life of the world to come. We long to hear the words of Jesus, "Well done good and faithful servant" (Matthew 25:23).

Think about These Things

Take some time to reflect on what you have just read in this chapter, then use the bulleted points below to prayerfully apply these biblical principles to your life and circumstances.

- On a piece of paper, or in a journal, write out your feelings. Perhaps you will say something like this: "How can I adjust to my new normal? I've settled into first this situatoin, and then into that situation. It's like it was with Joseph--first I am sold into slavery, then I end up in prison. How am I going to get to grips with this feelig of being forgotten? How can I manage these deep feelings of disappointment?"
- Consider the sovereignty of God, He's declared His love for you. He is a King who is both willing and able to help you and deliver you. While you are not in the most ideal situation currently, where can you discern His tender mercies ?.
- Who do you know that you can reach out today with a word of encouragement that God has not forgotten them and that the Lord is active although not immediately perceptible?
- Reflection point: The hymn writer, William Cowper, went through repeated episodes of depression and even considered taking his own life. Reflect prayerfully on the words he composed in the hymn *God Moves in a Mysterious Way*.

God moves in a mysterious way
His wonders to perform:
He plants His footsteps in the sea,
And rides upon the storm.

Deep in unfathomable mines
Of never-failing skill,
He treasures up His bright designs,
And works His sovereign will.

Ye fearful saints, fresh courage take;
The clouds ye so much dread
Are big with mercy, and shall break
In blessings on your head.

Judge not the Lord by feeble sense,
But trust Him for His grace;
Behind a frowning providence
He hides a smiling face.

His purposes will ripen fast,
Unfolding every hour:
The bud may have a bitter taste,
But sweet will be the flower.

Blind unbelief is sure to err,
And scan His work in vain;
God is His own Interpreter,
And He will make it plain.

- Read and reflect on Psalm 72.
- Now that you have read this chapter, as you reflect prayerfully on your situation, what is the main challenge you consider you are facing? What one thing can you do today, in light of what you have read in this chapter, can you commit to doing?

Section 3: Healing and Reconciliation

When you rise from the pit, what comes next? You never come out of the pit the same; you are changed by the experience. Your perspective is changed and you see life differently. The pit challenges your presuppositions about life and God. Your theological understanding is challenged. Life is never the same afterwards.

Joseph has finally been rescued from his time in prison. It has been a long journey through many trials over many years. From the time his brothers sought to kill him (but instead threw him in a pit) until the time he asked to be remembered by the cupbearer when he was released from jail, hoping against hope that he would be delivered from what he identified as an unjust pit, decades have passed. He no longer has any contact with his past. He has not seen his family for almost longer than he can remember.

He had started his journey as a spoiled younger brother beloved of his father and hated by his siblings. Now he has ended up being seated in the high courts of Pharoah's Egypt over the famine-relief effort. He has been given power over all of Egypt under Pharoah. He has been given a woman who has borne him two sons, the first named Manasseh, "For God has made me forget all my hardship and my father's house," and the second named Ephraim, "For God has made me fruitful in the land of my affliction." These names are significant and revealing.

At the end of his trial, Joseph wanted nothing to do with his family. He was moving on. He no longer wanted to remember what he had just gone through. He was now successful in the place when just a short time ago had been a place of affliction. He was angry with his brothers and his family and wanted nothing to do with them. He wanted to forget about them. But at the same time, he was thanking God for his newfound success. There was simultaneously anger against those who had put him through the trial, and thankfulness to God for where he ended up.

In our sinful, state two emotions can dwell together at the same time. Not knowing the plan of God from the beginning, Joseph blamed his brothers for starting this trial by throwing him in the pit and selling him off as a slave. At the end of his trial, he could rightfully thank God for delivering him and prospering him in his new position of power in Egypt, the place that had at firstbrought him so much affliction.

What Joseph failed to recognize was that it was all in the plan of God from the beginning. His trials were the means God chose to use to save the family and move the promise to Abraham further down the line.

Joseph still had much to learn. He would have to come to a place of forgiveness for his brothers. He would come to learn that God truly is in every situation working for his good. God was with Joseph every step of the way.

In the pit, there may be reason to blame others. There is certainly guilt to go around, but that cannot be our concern. If God is leading us, then we need to learn that in every situation we are to give thanks, as Paul tells us, for this is the will of God for us (see 1 Thessalonians 5:18).

God choose Joseph and put him in his position of power in order to save the children of Israel—the fruit of the promise to Abraham. In order for Joseph to fulfill the task God had given him to do, he would first have to learn to forgive those who had sinned against him, his brothers. As we will see, it was not an easy task. The trauma of all that he had gone through needed to be worked out in his life before he could come to the place where he could say that all that he had gone through had been the will of God for him.

We go through what we go through for a purpose. We learn to trust God and get a better look at ourselves, as God prepares us for ministry in his divine plan. In order to go forward, we need to learn to forgive, do good, and not seek revenge. All of that needs to be left in the hands of God.

Section 3: Healing and Reconciliation

6

Coming Out of the Pit

The time in a pit changes everything. Joseph would remain in prison for two more years after the cupbearer was restored to his position under Pharoah. His hope of being released when the cupbearer spoke with Pharoah died when it became apparent that he had been forgotten by him. Sometimes the pit gets so dark it seems hopeless. After all that he has been through, to realize his best chance of being set free had passed, Joesph now knew he was left with nothing. Over and over, God would seem to reach out to him with the promise of deliverance—only then to have his situation worsen.

The Long Trials

It's the long trials, the extended times in the pit, that begin to wear you out. It's when you go from one situation to another with no relief, with no guarantee that things will ever get better, that you need to hold on to the promise of God—the promise that he will never leave you or forsake you. That is the one promise you can rely upon when you don't understand what you are going through. It is simple and direct, and it depends on nothing you can do. Jesus is with us on the mountaintop and in the deepest pit. When there is no place to go to and no one to turn to, we are left with the words of Jesus: "And lo, I am with you always even till the end of the age" (see Matthew 28:20).

William Cowper, in his hymn *God Moves in A Mysterious Way*, writes,

> *Blind unbelief is sure to err, and scan his work in vain;*
> *God is his own interpreter, and he will make it plain.*
> *You fearful saints, fresh courage take; The clouds you so much dread,*
> *are big with mercy and will break with blessings on your head.*

Joseph had to learn this truth. There is no answer that he could see as a reason for lingering in his prison cell. There was no logic to justify his situation. Anyone looking from the outside would have been wrong in his evaluation. Job's associates thought they understood their friend's condition, yet they were completely incorrect. Search as we will for the reasons for the situations we find ourselves in, and it is likely we will be wrong. We will often scan God's works in vain. It is God who interprets his own acts; it the greater plan of God that remains unseen to us most of the time.

Two years after the cupbearer had been reestablished, Pharoah had two dreams that no one could interpret. In the first, he was standing by the Nile, and he saw seven plump healthy cows come out of the river; after that, seven thin, ugly cows came out of the river and ate the healthy cows. In the second dream he saw seven ears of plump, healthy grain growing on one stalk; after that, the seven ears of blighted thin ears of grain swallowed up the seven plump ears. What could these possibly mean? Pharoah called all his magicians and wisemen, but no one was able interpret the dreams. But God moves in mysterious ways. The cupbearer suddenly remembered that some guy he had met in prison, Joseph, had interpreted his dream for him. Pharoah ordered Joseph to be brought before him immediately.

Turning Point

This was the turning point in Joseph's life. God had brought him to this place. Everything he had gone through was in preparation for this moment. He was to be brought before Pharoah, where God would give him the interpretation of his dreams. The plan of God was unfolding. All Joseph had gone through was the process where God was bringing him to this place where he would be in a position of power to save his family, the children of Israel, from the famine and move the promise forward—the wonderful promise of God given to Abraham.

After Joseph had interpreted the dreams, Pharoah placed him over a strategic famine-relief program. He would be responsible to gather grain and store it during the good years and to distribute it during the years of famine. Pharoah also gave Joseph a wife named Asenath who gave him two sons. What he named the boys tells us much about where Joseph was at. He named his first son Manasseh, "For God has made me forget all my hardship and all my father's house" (Genesis 41:51). His second son he named Ephraim, "For God has made me fruitful in the land of my affliction" (v. 52). Joseph was ready to forget his past and move on with his life.

However, God was not ready to let Jospeh move on, as there were some things he had to deal with. What he had gone through was traumatic. His family had rejected him and had wanted to do away with him. One thing led to another as he went from bad to worse. He was angry with his family. Now he declared that God had made him forget his affliction and his family. He believed his past was past.

More time elapsed. There were the seven years of prosperity before the seven years of famine. Then something happened: Because God was not finished with Joseph, there needed to be reconciliation. The purpose of Joseph's trials was to save his family. There would have to be a reuniting of the family, a healing of old wounds. At some point, Jacob learned there was grain for sale in Egypt. He sent ten of his sons to go buy grain so the family could survive. He keept Benjamin behind. Benjamin was the second son of his favorite wife who had died in childbirth. He had lost Joseph; he was not going to lose Benjamin.

When the Problem People Show Up

Then, one thing Joseph had never thought would happen did happen. One day, his brothers showed up before him, asking to purchase food. How would he handle it? All that he had tried to avoid, all he had prayed to God to remove, to put behind him once and for all so that he could finally move on, came rushing back to him in one brief encounter. His brothers who had started all of his troubles were now before him asking for his help—the help only he could provide.

Often the challenges that the pit brings to us—those moments of growth and spiritual development, of learning to lean on God when there is nowhere else to turn and no one else to lean upon—do not end just because we are out of the pit. There were other lessons for Joseph to learn. If it was God who had led him to the pit—just as Jesus was led into the wilderness by the Spirit to be tempted by the devil—and he couldn't just write his brothers off and, in a real sense, send them away hungry. He had been placed by God in a position to serve those in need because of the famine, and that included especially his brothers who were God's chosen people. Joseph would have to come to grips with his anger. He would have to learn to forgive so that he could move on with what God had called him to do.

Who Is to Blame?

Whatever the reason for our struggles, it is always easy to put the blame on someone else and not take any ownership for our part in the situation. Sometimes we want to blame others, sometimes we blame God, or maybe just circumstances or fate. But coming out of the pit is just as much a learning experience as going through it.

Joseph could blame his brothers—and they were certainly responsible—but he had some culpability as well. His arrogance toward them from his favorite-son position contributed also, though it did not excuse their hatred for him. We are not responsible for how others treat us, but we are responsible for our treatment of them. "Do unto others as you would have them do to you" is the golden rule (see Matthew 7:12). We are to treat others as we want to be treated—and our actions should not be directed by how they treat us. We are to love our enemies and do good to them (see Matthew 5:43). Sometimes coming out of the pit causes us to reevaluate our attitudes toward others. Do our actions reflect the values of the kingdom of God or are they the values of this world? Joseph had some things to learn.

When Joseph's brothers appear before him, he recognizes them immediately. He doesn't rejoice over the fact that they are there; he treats them as strangers and speaks harshly to them. Joseph is dealing with some anger issues. He is not ready to receive his brothers. Perhaps he had just thanked God that he was moving past his trials and was putting them and his family behind him. When they show up, he is being forced to address what he no longer wanted to face.

Often when you come out of a long trial, your initial response is to put it behind and move on. You try to forget the hurt and the struggle, and just start afresh. Joseph wanted to do just that but God wouldn't let him because the resolution was part of the reason for the trial in the first place.

As his brothers stood before him, Joseph recollected his dreams. God was about to reveal to him the plan behind the events. Joseph was beginning to realize that the dreams and all that had followed were all part of God's divine plan for him and his family. Yet he still wanted them to pay them back for what they had done to him. He accused them of being spies. They denied it and identified themselves as honest men. They were scared. They told him they were his servants and were the children of one man. There were ten of them present, as Joseph could see, but the youngest was at home with their father and one other son was no longer. They said nothing more about Joseph.

Getting Even?

Joseph wanted to see his younger brother again, but he also wanted to make the brothers suffer for what they had done to him. He was starting to understand that what had happened to him was the fulfillment of his dream, but that didn't take away his anger and desire for some revenge on his part. He directed them to send one of them to bring back their brother, while the rest would be put in jail. Joseph wanted to give them a taste of what they had done to him. He ended up putting them all in jail for three days to think about their response to him. On the third day, he changed the offer. They were all to return to get the younger brother—but with the exception of one of them who would remain in custody.

God was now speaking to the brothers. They talked among themselves and admitted that what was happening to them was because they were guilty for what they had done to Joseph. They vividly remembered the distressed look on Joseph's face as they handed him over to the Ishmaelites. Reuben reminded them that he had told them not to hurt Joseph. They were learning this principle: your sin will find you out (see Numbers 32:23). They could see this as punishment for what they had done. Nearby, Joseph was listening to them speak, although they didn't know he could understand them.

Joseph himself was going to have to come to grips with all that was unfolding before him. The brothers knew what they had done to him was wrong and God was not pleased with them. Joseph knew what they were dealing with, but they had as yet said nothing to him. Joseph was not ready to let the brothers off the hook for what they had done, yet he struggled with his emotions. Hearing his brothers, Joseph had to turn away from them for he started to weep.

Simeon was taken and bound before the brothers. This added to their fear. Joseph was conflicted. After taking Simeon as a kind of punishment for the brothers, he filled their sacks with provisions, returned the money they had brought as payment, and gave them food for their journey home. Joseph wanted to punish his brothers and yet also bless them at the same time. It is hard to distance ourselves from our circumstances and just leave things in the hands of God. God was working on the brothers and on Joseph. They were all going to learn to trust God in every situation. They were to learn that God is a God of mercy and grace.

On the journey home, the brothers realized their money had been returned to them. They interpreted it as a punishment by God for what they had done to Joseph all those years ago. On returning to their father, Jacob, they told him what had happened to them, that their money had been returned. Moreover, Simeon had been put in prison, and it was a condition that Benjamin was to be taken to Egypt or Simeon would not be released. Jacob sensed trouble. He had lost Joseph and Simeon, and now he could lose Benjamin. The chaos of his dysfunctional family was pressing on him in his old age. Reuben even offered to Jacob that he could kill his own two sons if he failed to bring Benjamin back.

There is just so much wrong with this. Imagine the son telling his father that he may kill his two grandsons if he doesn't return from Egypt with his father's favorite son. But Jacob has not changed. He refuses to let Benjamin go with Reuben. His reason? One son is dead—Joseph—and Benjamin is the only son left. If he is lost, Jacob will go in sorrow to his grave.

This whole account demonstrates the fruit of a dysfunctional family. Jacob has a favorite wife Rachel, a favorite son, Joseph, and now there is a favorite son, Benjamin. He has no regard for his other children. Jacob has some things to learn, as well.

Everything remains on hold, but God is not done with this family. The famine continues and they again start to run out of food. Jacob tells his sons to return to Egypt to buy more food and Judah reminds him that they cannot return without their younger brother, so Judah promises to take care of Benjamin and bring him back safely. It is finally agreed that they may go. They bring presents from the land, hoping to soften the Egyptian's heart and not hurt their younger brother.

Others in the Pit. . .

We now turn our attention away from Joseph's struggles to those of his family members. They are finding themselves in their own version of a pit. Jacob does not treat his family well. He has favorites, and he does not hide this. His two wives had fought over his affection and four women eventually got involved in the making of Jacob's family. He had chosen to show favor on the sons of his favorite wife. Rachel had only given Jacob two sons, Joseph and Benjamin, and in fact she had died in childbirth as Benjamin was being delivered. Consider how Jacob had lost Joseph, Rachel, and now he would possibly lose Benjamin.

How does Jacob move on? The brothers wrestle with their own sin, having sold Joseph into slavery and having lied to their father about what had happened. They are now feeling the hand of God upon them. They sense that they are experiencing the judgment of God for what they had done. God is now bringing everything out into the open. Each person involved is going to learn to trust in God and receive his grace, mercy, and forgiveness.

There will be a few more trips to Egypt. Joseph will, on the one hand, try to punish his brothers, and, on the other hand, bless them. The brothers return this time with Benjamin. Jacob is left behind to sorrow over the loss of his children. God leaves him to think about the condition of his life and family. He has many regrets.

Reunion and Revelation

Back in Egypt, when Joseph sees Benjamin, he decides to meet with his brothers in his own house. This strikes fear in their hearts. They see it as a trap because of the money that had been put into their sacks. They tell the steward of Joseph's house what had happened, and he tells them God must have put the money there, for he had been paid in full for the food they had taken. Simeon is released and brought out to them. When Joseph arrives, they are presented before him, and he asks about Jacob. Upon seeing Benjamin, his compassion grows warm for his brothers. He leaves their company so they do not see him weeping. God is moving on Joseph's heart. He joins them and food is served, with Benjamin getting a bigger portion. Joseph does not eat at the same table because Egyptians are not permitted to eat with Hebrews.

Though he was beginning to soften toward his brothers, he was not done with them yet. He filled their sacks with food, replaced their money, and in Benjamin's sack he instructed his servants to put his silver cup. The brothers then headed out on their journey home. After a short time, Joseph sent his steward after them and accused them of stealing from Joseph, as his golden cup had gone missing. The brothers had no idea what the steward was talking about, for, surely, they had taken nothing. They were so convinced of their innocence that they told him that whichever person's sack had the cup should be put to death. The cup was found in Benjamin's sack. The brothers immediately understood what they had done. Their situation had just become much worse. If Benjamin were to be killed, what would they tell their father? They would be the reason for the death of two of Jacob's children. As the narrative develops, they went back to Egypt and were brought before Joseph, who then questioned them about the missing cup.

Finally, Judah lays out the whole story. Their father is old. His wife, who has died, has left him two sons; one is dead and the young one is all that he has left. If they return without the youngest son, the father will die. Judah begs for mercy.

Dealing with the Coverup

There has been a lot of covering up in this account. The brothers were hoping they could somehow move on with their lives after Joseph, but God would not allow this. God was bringing healing to the whole family. Jacob was holding on to the last bit of his life that he deemed important. He seemed to only care for Rachel and her children. God kept removing them from his life. Joseph had to deal with all that his family had put him through, and it was a real struggle for him. He wanted healing but he also wanted some revenge—some satisfaction in seeing his brothers pay for what they had done. God was in all of this, working for the good of the members of this family. As the story unfolded, each one's sins was revealed and brought into focus. God was allowing them to feel the weight of what they had done to each other. That, in and of itself, would make this an important lesson for us. But there is more.

Upon hearing Judah, Joseph clears the house so he is left alone with his brothers. He reveals to them who he is—their brother, Joseph, whom they had sold into slavery. He tells them not to be distressed or angry with themselves. He announces the grace of God to them, saying, in effect: "You sold me to Egypt but it was God who sent me here. This is the plan of God revealed. People do things, and some appear to be bad and have uncertain results, but behind those events is the hand of God moving us to his appointed end." When we end up in a pit, there is much to learn about ourselves; there might be sin to repent of, but the important question to ask is what God is doing, and how he is using me for his greater good.

Joseph has come to realize that God had sent him ahead of his brothers for their good, to save them from the famine. What's a key principle that emerges from this? One is that the struggles we go through might really be for the good of others. Jesus laid down his life for us. He calls us to follow him. As we do, we put the needs of others before ourselves. God uses us for the common good.

Joseph went through a lot. God was teaching him many things, but ultimately God was using Joseph to accomplish the greater good of saving his people.

As matters transpire, things go well with the family. Joseph establishes his relatives in Goshen, and everything seems to be put behind them. But our fears die hard, and when Jacob dies, the brothers begin to wonder if Joseph really is still angry with them. Had he just been kind to them for Jacob's sake? They once again send a message to Joseph, confessing their sin for what they had done to him.

Joseph had come to the place that we all must come to when wrestling with our pit situations. He tells them, "Do not fear, for am I in the place of God? As for you, you meant evil against me, but God meant it for good, to bring it about that many people should be kept alive, as they are today. . ." (see Genesis 50:20). Joseph knew he was where God would have him to be. It's very important for you to understand that Joseph doesn't let his brothers off the hook by telling them not to worry about it. He puts it in these kinds of terms: "Don't fear me, I'm good. You meant it for evil!" He understood that, but also that God meant it for good. There was no personal judgment on his part. He understood completely clearly what had happened and the feelings of those involved, but he could see, too, that there was something greater happening: God was at work saving his people! Any feelings of anger or a desire for revenge were gone. He was in the will of God, and he no longer felt responsible for what had happened.

When we come to the place where we can say God is in my situation working for good, then we are free to walk in the grace and mercy of God.

Think about These Things

Take some time to reflect on what you have just read in this chapter, then use the bulleted points below to prayerfully apply these biblical principles to your life and circumstances.

- On a piece of paper, or in a journal, write out your feelings. Perhaps you will say something like this: "I feel like I have gotten out of my pit, but there is still a whole lot of stuff I have to navigate. Why can't I just put my old life behind me? Why do I have these ongoing reminders of my past when all I want to do is move on and forget it? How can I deal with my anger and frustration over these things?"
- Consider these questions: In which ways have you changed because of your time of having been in the pit? Can you submit to the reality that the Lord wanted for you to fall into the pit in the first place? Can you embrace the truth that, even when you were in the pit, there the loving hand of God was sustaining you?
- List three or more ways that your pit has not only changed you, but your perspective about God. How has it changed your outlook on others, especially if they were the causes of your suffering?
- Commit to spending time in prayer. In forgiveness, see if you can release those that may have caused you to suffer. And tell the Lord that you will never hold it against him. Praise and give thanks to him for being in the pit with you throughout the time you spent there.
- Reflection point: God doesn't give you moral laws and rules only, but also gives you a relationship with Jesus to help you overcome and give you rest even when you can't figure things out related to the pit.
- Read and reflect on Matthew 11:28-30.
- Now that you have read this chapter, as you reflect prayerfully on your situation, what is the main challenge you consider you are facing? What one thing can you do today, in light of what you have read in this chapter, can you commit to doing?

7

What We Have Learned

We have have been on a journey with our father in the faith, Joseph. During this time, we have been looking at (and thinking about) our own stories. We live in a fallen world. Our focus is usually on the world *as it should be*, but we live in the world *as it is*. The world as it should be is just and fair; the good guy is always rewarded and evil is always punished.

A Gospel that Prospers?

Often, we are presented with a gospel that is not really good news at all—promises of the good life, a life of prosperity that is virtually stress free. Give your life to Jesus, follow him, and he will answer all of life's struggles. In the world as it should be, everything works out with little struggle on our part. Life is clear and simple. Good is good and bad is bad and there are no gray areas. God rewards the good and punishes the evil. If only life was so easy and predictable!

We live in the world as it is. Often justice seems far away. Life appears to be unfair. As Christians, the struggles we face are common to ordinary people. The rain falls on the just and the unjust. As followers of Jesus, we face the same struggles as those outside the faith. Every area of our lives is tainted with sin. A simple scan of the lives of our mothers and fathers in the faith reveals the truth that we all have fallen short of the glory of God.

I chose to look at the account of Joseph because it addresses many of the concerns and questions we all face. At the beginning of the book, the question was raised about an individual's worthiness to be used by God. If my theological understanding tells me only the worthy are in a position to be used by God, that he can only use good people, then all of us are eliminated.

Joseph's situation raises a number of questions for us. The

biblical text doesn't necessarily give us clear and definitive answers to the questions we have concerning the situations, the pits, we find ourselves in. But the biblical text does give us insight into the nature of God. It assures us that God is in control of all things, that our lives are not adrift in an unjust world. God has a plan, and he is accomplishing his good and perfect will for each of us as he is bringing to fruition his divine purpose to redeem his fallen creation. Joseph's story is a story of hope and assurance of the love of God toward his people in the midst of confusing and, at times, very challenging situations.

Messed Up because of the Fall

Can God use broken and sinful people? Who are the people of this story? The family in this story are the children of Jacob who had his name changed to Israel. This family consists of the children of Israel or better known throughout the Scriptures as the people of God. They were chosen by him to be used to reveal God to the nations.

When we read the genealogy of Jesus, we like to point out that Jesus has people like Rahab the harlot in his ancestry. The fact is that Jesus is descended from this dysfunctional family of Israel. This hateful, divided family is the family God chose to play a major role in his divine plan of redemption. Can we be used by God? The answer is yes, most certainly!

We look at ourselves and we see our shortcomings and we ask ourselves how God could possibly use us. Paul understood our struggle. In Romans 7, he writes of the war that daily takes place within him. He continues to do what is wrong and fails to do what is right. "Who will deliver me from this body of death?" he asks (see Romans 7:25). He then thanks God for Jesus Christ. Writing of his life in another passage, 1 Timothy 1:15, he declares that Jesus died for sinners—of whom he himself is the chief.

God uses broken people. Scripture is clear and covers up nothing. Everyone God uses is broken. Pick one—Paul, Peter, Abraham, Jacob, Joseph, Mary—any one of them. All have sinned and all fall short of the glory of God. They all cling to the mercy of God, but they are all broken sinner-saints.

Can God use you? The answer is yes. The promise to the believer is that Jesus will never leave us or forsake us. The blood of Jesus Christ cleanses us from all sin (see 1 John 1:7-9). We are being conformed to the image of Jesus, but we are not there yet. The Joseph story reminds us that God uses broken people for his purposes.

God Can Bring Good from Bad

Another thing we learn is that God is in every situation working for the good of those who love him and are called according to his purposes. He takes bad situations and turns them for his glory.

The situation in Joseph's family got so bad that the hatred for him reached a height where the brothers were willing to kill him to make it stop. It went way beyond sibling rivalry. They were willing to lie to their father and kill their brother to satisfy the hatred they had toward him.

As you look upon this situation, you would ask whether anything good could come out of this family. How often do you ask if anything good could come out of your situation? Scripture always has an answer for the questions of our life—and Scripture's answer is often followed on by the words "But God. . ."

What we so often fail to see as the story unfolds is the invisible hand of God. Joseph's brothers plan his death, Reuben persuades them not to kill him, and they end up selling him to the Ishmaelites who, in turn, sell him as a slave to Potiphar in Egypt. You could say that God protected his life by preventing his brothers from killing him, but is that really a satisfying answer? Surely, if God is a loving God, he has to do more than just keep Joseph alive! As the story progresses, we see Joseph's life deteriorate, going from bad to worse.

So the question remains: "Where is God in all of this?"

It is the same question people have asked throughout the book.

- Why did this happen to me?
- Why am I in this situation?
- Why am I sick, and why doesn't God heal me?

Where Are the Answers?

We so want an answer to that question. Our minds cannot live with uncertainty. There has to be a reason. So, we blame ourselves. We must have done something wrong to deserve this. Rather than clinging to the mercy of God, we look for reasons. There has to be a logical reason for what is happening.

But, too often the god we worship is not the God of the Bible. He is a god of judgment who punishes us for our shortcomings and sins. He is not the God who, because of his love and grace in Jesus, casts our sins as far as the east is from the west and remembers them no more (Psalm 103:12). So we struggle with our circumstances, trying to find a reason why and also find a way to appease this angry god.

Part of our problem is that we don't know the whole story. We are finite beings with limited understanding. God does not reveal to us all things, as we would be incapable of understanding. God is simply telling us to trust him and not to lean on our own understanding (Proverbs 3:5-6). That turns out to be a big ask. Like Job, we want answers. So, Joseph's story reminds us that behind the world we see and experience is a God who has a plan that he is bringing to fruition.

Just as in our kinds of experiences, Joseph goes through a series of events: He is sold into slavery, falsely accused of rape, and faces imprisonment and rejection. Often our situations deteriorate as well. Sometimes we fall into a pit. We have faith, yet nothing changes. The decisions of others cause us to have to deal with the consequences of our decisions for the rest of our life, and sometimes things just go from bad to worse. We think our situation will change, but nothing seems to happen. And then when our situation does change, we fall into another pit. "What is going on?" we cry. "Where is God?"

In those situations, like Joseph we settle in to our new normal and try and serve God the best we can, but the questions never go away.

- Why is this happening to me?
- What have I done wrong?
- I believe, so why is my faith not working?
- Where is God?

Has this been your experience?

Managing the "New Normal"

Joseph declines in stages. At each stage of his decline, he learns to adjust to his new normal and, in fact, God prospers him. But what God doesn't do is to deliver Joseph! Sold to Potiphar, Joseph serves him as he serves the Lord, and God blesses the house of Potiphar. Joseph is placed over the whole house.

Perhaps he thought, "I'm not sure why I am here," but he settled in and made the best of a bad situation. When he was accused of rape, Potiphar had him thrown in jail. Perhaps he thought, "I'm not sure what God is doing," but he served God to the best of his ability and so the jailer put him in charge of the other prisoners. Again, he adjusted to his new normal. But is there a purpose to all of this?

John's Experience

John is not healed from his accident. He has cried out to God over and over for years. Well-intentioned Christians have told him to just "have faith." He does have faith. But through it all, although he has held on to God, God has not healed him. But God has deepened his faith. Like Job, John hasn't get answers to his questions but he has learned that God is always with him. It's been a struggle at times because the theology he was taught didn't line up with the experiences God has brought him through.

Our mind wants answers but God is calling us to a relationship with him. He has called John to trust him when there are no answers or when the answers are not satisfying.

Sharon's Experience

Throughout her life, Sharon has fallen into and climbed out of many pits. She had tuberculosis, quadruple bypass heart surgery, and breast cancer. Over the years, well-meaning Christians have tried to offer reasons for her suffering all in an attempt to—in their mind—cover for God. When our theological grid doesn't fit the map with the real situation, we want to make excuses for God. Instead of saying we don't know what God is doing, we come up with some story to cover for him. So, for example, after she had experienced a miscarriage, Sharon's pastor told her that "God had taken away the baby because he knew it would grow up to be a criminal." Somehow that covered for a situation that had no good answer.

Faulty Reasoning

God doesn't want (or need) our faulty reasoning. We need to learn to let God be God and let him reveal to us his greater plan. In the memorble words of the hymn writer, William Cowper,

> *God is his own interpreter,*
> *and he will make it plain.*

Both John and Sharon have gotten bad advice from good Christians. Both have learned through their trials that it is God who holds them—and it's certainly not the other way round!

God has a purpose for the things he allows us to go through. He is in every situation working for our good. Joseph had to get to Egypt, into Pharoah's court, and into a position of power so that he could save his family from the famine. And he had to learn to forgive his brothers for what they had done to him. He also had to learn to walk humbly before God. Trials have a way of doing that.

As the favorite son, Joseph was arrogant and boastful. As a slave, he had little room for pride, and even less so as a prisoner. Joseph was humbled so that he could learn to walk in humility. So while at the beginning Joseph had boasted about what he heard from God in his dreams and about how his family would bow down before him, that was one of the main reasons his brothers hated him and turned against him.

After being dragged from pit to pit until he was finally exalted, Joseph knew it there was nothing in him, and that whatever he experienced was as a result of God's dealings with him.

Finally. . .

Joseph's final lesson came when, after being lifted up in Egypt, his brothers showed up looking for help. Only he could help them. In the background, his youngest brother and his father were part of the need. Life is complicated! Coming to realize that he was being used by God to save his family, he had to come to the place where he could see that everything that had happened to him was all in the plan of God. He was there to save his family from the famine. He had to learn to forgive his brothers.

Joseph ended up in the place that we all must come through as we journey with Jesus. He was content to know that he was in the place that God wanted him to be. He didn't excuse his brothers; they would have to answer to God. What he did say was that he forgave them and did not hold against them what they had done to him. He came to the place where he could rest in the arms of God, no matter what the outcome. That is the position of faith.

Consider Jesus

There is a moment in the life of Jesus that illustrates this point. Jesus was preaching in Nazareth. There, the people become enraged by his teaching and attempted to walk him off a cliff. They pushed him to the edge of the precipice, yet we are told that Jesus turned and walked through the crowd (see Luke 4:30). It wasn't his time yet. As we are being conformed to the image of Jesus, we need to learn to come to the place in our struggles to rest in the hands of God, knowing nothing will happen to us that is not in the wise plan of God.

If I lose my investments, can I say words such as these? "The LORD gives and the LORD takes, blessed be the name of the LORD" (see Job 1:21). If my life is altered through an accident, can I rest in the divine providence of God, trusting that there is a greater good in my suffering? In chronic sickness, can I learn to trust in a loving Savior who has allowed all this for the greater good?

We want to be like God, knowing all things. But we can't. We are finite beings who cannot comprehend all things. We are also fallen creatures who see, at best, through a dim glass. Let me repeat: God has chosen that the just shall live by faith. He doesn't reveal all things to us. He doesn't answer all of our questions and satisfy our curiosity. What he does do is walk with us. He teaches us to trust him through our experiences. Christianity is not an intellectual pursuit. To be a Christian does not mean that you memorize a list of doctrines, rules, and laws. A Christian is someone who is in a living and ongoing relationship with Jesus. Christians are not people who know about God; rather, they are people who know God.

You might be a student of history and know a lot about great and important historical figures. But what you can't say is that you know the person. The only people you can say that you know are people you have experiences with, people you have walked with.

We learn to know God when he walks with us through the ups and downs of our life. We meet God in the pits of our lives. It is only coming out of a pit that we, like Joseph, can say, "What you have meant for evil, God intended for God" (see Genesis 50:20).

Think about These Things

Take some time to reflect on what you have just read in this chapter, then use the bulleted points below to prayerfully apply these biblical principles to your life and circumstances.

- On a piece of paper, or in a journal, write out your feelings. Perhaps you will say something like this: "I'm at the point where things are more settled; I see the hand of God at work, bringing good outcomes even when there have been evil forces at work through people close to me. I have learned very real lessons in my pit, and I am somehow the better for it. But I really do need the ongoing grace of God in my life if I am to remain effective in his service and in relation to my family, friends, and others."
- Consider these questions: Have you experienced evil and the are you facing the tension between the world as you think it should be as opposed to how the world really is? What are the emotions you are dealing with, and do you have a plan, after reading this book, to be reconciled with the purpose and providence of God?
- When you are in a state of contentment with God's pruposes, it leads you to to be reconciled with others. You cannot be reconciled with others unless you are first at peace with God.
- Take a moment to thank the Lord, no matter how difficult it might be, for how bad things have turned for your good. Use this as a new stage of spiritual growth and an open door for ministry to others who are in a pit. Pray for people you know who have gone down into a pit, and consider sending them an email or calling them to tell them that, though they have yet to see it, there is resolution to their trial and encourage them to keep their faith firmly in God.
- Read and reflect on Psalm 16:6 (KJV) and Psalm 50:14,15
- Now that you have read this chapter, as you reflect prayerfully on your situation, what is the main challenge you consider you are facing? What one thing can you do today, in light of what you have read in this chapter, can you commit to doing?

Epilogue: Final Perspectives

We long to live in an ordered world— place where good is rewarded and evil punished. The world God created in the beginning, out of the chaos, as seen in Genesis 1, was such a world. At the end of the creation, God declared that what he had made was very good. God built into his creation an order of how things should run. But something happened: sin entered into the world and death reigned. The ground no longer yielded to man's labor. Weeds appeared and labor became characterized by toil and struggle. The creation groaned for the redemption of God.

Order Versus Disorder

An ordered world makes sense to us. There are rules and things happen in predictable ways. The lines of good and evil are clear. Since there is a just and moral foundation to the created order, most of the time things work out in ways that are understandable to us. We work hard and we are rewarded for our efforts. We treat people nicely and they respond in like manner. Good triumphs over evil. Our lives proceed as planned until they don't. Sin takes place and we find ourselves in situations beyond our control and, more than that, beyond our understanding. What then?

We have been journeying with Joseph. When we met him, his life was good. His family was a mess, but he was the favorite son of the favorite wife. He was spoiled by his father, who gave him an expensive coat of many colors. His brothers had no place for him but his father covered for him. His life was going well until it wasn't. When the timing and the opportunity was right, his brothers sold him into slavery. Sin takes place.

John was going through his life and everything was fine until he fell from the tree. Steve's plans were falling into place until the economy crashed. Mary planned for her future until her kidney failed. Sharon was enjoying retirement until she heard the dreadful word—cancer.

As we walked with Joseph, his life continually worsened until he found himself in an Egyptian prison. Oftentimes we are caught by surprise by the events of our life because we don't live in the conscious awareness that we live in a fallen world. We too often walk around self-deceived, thinking the ordered world will act as expected. But pits are inevitable. We all find ourselves in one at some point in our lives. We learn a lot from Joseph's story.

Learning the Lessons

Joseph learned to adapt to each situation he found himself in. When we find ourselves in a pit, we must learn to continue to serve God. As we walk in the awareness that our world is fallen, we learn to appreciate and take comfort in God's presence. The gospel is God's answer to our sinful world. The good news is that God, in Christ, came down and dwelt among us. Jesus' promise is that he would never leave us or forsake us. We might get caught unawares when we stumble into a pit, yet we can take comfort in the fact that, no matter how bad it gets, we are tethered to God through Jesus. Joseph was never outside of the will of God, and neither are we.

Another thing that we learn from the Joseph story is that God has a plan, and he is accomplishing his purpose through us. God's plan is the redemption of creation and the salvation of his people. We wait for the resurrection of the dead and we wait for the life of the world to come. In Joseph's story, God was moving the promise forward that he had made to Abraham. To do that, he had to get Joseph into the court of Pharoah. All that Joseph went through was to get him to the place where God could use him to save his people and move the promise.

We don't know the plans of God or our role in them. We are not called to know; we are called to trust and follow. At the end of his struggles, Joseph learned that it was the work of God that got him to the position he was in. His brothers had their evil intentions but God used them for his good.

To quote William Cowper the hymnwriter once more:

Epilogue: Final Perspectives

You fearful saints, fresh courage take;
The clouds you so much dread
Are big with mercy and shall break
In blessings on your head."

We are fearful of the unknown. Our minds have a hard time settling when things are unclear. We look for answers when oftentimes there are no answers. Cowper exhorts us to take courage, for the things we fear, the things we dread, are in fact filled with the mercy of God. If our faith is in a merciful God, we have nothing to fear. In our darkest hour, he holds our hand. Nothing shall separate us from the love of God. The God who sent his Son to die for us will not lead us into harm's way and then desert us in our time of need. What we go through is for our own benefit and for the furtherance of the plan of God. In the New Testament, Paul reminds us that he had learned to be content in every situation (see Philippians 4:11), and so, too, should we.

My prayer is that this journey has been helpful in your walk with the Lord. James tells us to count it all joy when we fall into diverse temptations or trials. God is working on us, conforming us to the image of Jesus. Don't be discouraged but put your trust in Jesus, for he cares for you. God uses broken people and, at times, leads them through difficult and trying times. Don't be discouraged; his love for you is sure. You might not always see the hand of God upholding you, but his love and mercy are sure and never failing.

How Did I Get into This Pit?

Made in the USA
Columbia, SC
09 July 2024

d1efd6e2-ebca-4d32-8878-a43a8c04d9deR02